Small Miracles

Extraordinary Coincidences
from Everyday Life

Yitta Halberstam
&
Judith Leventhal

ADAMS MEDIA CORPORATION
Holbrook, Massachusetts

To my sons Yossi and Eli—my own "small miracles." — YHM
To Jules and Arielle, my miracles of miracles. — JFL

Published by
Adams Media Corporation
260 Center Street, Holbrook, MA 02343

ISBN: 1-55850-646-2
Printed in the United States of America.

J I H G

Library of Congress Cataloging-in-Publication Data
Mandelbaum, Yitta Halberstam.
Small miracles : extraordinary coincidences from everyday life /
Yitta Halberstam Mandelbaum and Judith Frankel Leventhal.
p.   cm.
ISBN 1-55850-646-2 (pbk.)
1. Coincidence—Psychic aspects. I. Leventhal, Judith Frankel. II. Title.
BF1175.M36   1997
133.8—dc20   96-43249
CIP

Cover art by Barry David Marcus.

*This book is available at quantity discounts for bulk purchases.
For information, call 1-800-872-5627 (in Massachusetts, 617-767-8100).*

Visit our home page at http://www.adamsmedia.com

Preface
by Dr. Bernie Siegel

I'm writing a new book and it's coming to a close, and I want to conclude it with the words "The End." But suddenly, to my own surprise, an inner voice tells me, instead of writing "The End," to write "The Beginning." Hmm, I say to myself . . . well, that makes sense! Because if the people who are reading the book have read it well and absorbed its message, then hopefully, it will be the *beginning* of a new life for them!

But then I start to wonder . . . where did that impulse to write "The Beginning" come from? It wasn't in my plan; I know that. Something, or someone made me write it. Perhaps it was God.

Often, I don't know what I'm going to write until I see it down on paper. I used to find myself asking aloud: from God knows where did this come? Now, I know.

Once, when I was about four years old, I almost choked to death on a small toy that I had taken apart. I was alone in my room and no adult was nearby. So there I was choking, and suddenly, for no apparent reason, I vomited. The tiny parts of the toy came flying out and I could breathe. But later, I asked myself in amazement, "Now who did that? Who made me vomit? Was it God or an angel or spirit who entered the scene and made me vomit?"

But this book isn't about me, or about strange occurrences, or acts of fate or guilt or fault if no angel intercedes. It is about coincidences, the seemingly random acts that turn out not to be so random at all. How they happen, to whom, and why? Is God behind the orchestration of these "coincidences?"

I believe that *nothing* is a "coincidence." It's all part of creation and God's plan and our response. We just have to be open to seeing it. We have to want to see it and participate in creation. For example, when I was born, the man printing the birth certificate asked my parents my name. The name spoken was "Benzion — son of Shabsi," but the man transcribing it onto the birth certificate didn't understand the Hebrew name and created his own rendition of my name. Thus, my name, as it appears on the birth certificate, is "Shepherd." God had already determined my calling; to be a shepherd in the community as a spiritual, and intellectual, leader.

A common coincidence that I experience all the time is that I find pennies wherever I go. When I enter a hotel room for the first time and it's been freshly cleaned, vacuumed, spotless, I can often count on finding a penny on the threshold. In the airport, in a restaurant, even sitting atop my luggage, I'll suddenly spy one solitary penny. Now, what does that mean? What does it say on a penny? "In God We Trust." It's not the value of the money that's important, but its message, its wholeness —

a reminder that God is directing my energies, God is here and I am on my path.

Here's another example: My wife and I own a cat named Miracle, and we decided to get her some company. A neighbor's cat had a litter of kittens and we were invited to choose one of our liking. I brought an adorable-looking kitten back home, but he and my wife didn't hit it off. The match didn't work out, and I had to bring him back to the original owner. My wife was sorry but the owner assured us there was no problem, all the other kittens had already been adopted—all, that is, except one. Somehow, no one seemed to like this last one, because she had grown up in a barn, was dark-brown, and very fearful of people.

"Oh, what's her name?" I asked and the owner answered casually, "Penny." I hadn't been planning to try the experiment a second time, but the minute I heard the name, I knew it was right. So we adopted Penny and she and Miracle get along just fine. She was named Penny by a child who saw her being born and said, "She looks like a Penny."

So why do coincidences happen to some people and not to others? I believe that I look for coincidences in my life and have faith and so I find them. If you stay rooted in the intellect only, and disregard the spiritual aspects of life, you won't have them. If you learn to become more fully conscious, more aware of what's going on in your body and stop and listen to the universe, to keep journals, to write poetry, then coincidences will happen. Behave as if you have coincidences in your life, expect them, when you are ready to receive them, they'll come. You develop the intuitive in yourself.

This uses the exact same principle as "Behave as if you're the person you want to become," and that is whom you become! Once, I demonstrated this to a student of mine who was skeptical about our own ability to create coincidences. I was lecturing at a school an hour away from my home and when the lecture was over, I said to my student who rode back with me, "Watch this. I'm going to drive back home using an entirely different route than I ordinarily use, to show you something." Sure enough, about half a mile away from my home, I passed my wife driving her car, and she started waving and signaling. I rolled down my window and she said, "Oh, honey, I'm so glad to see you! I wanted to get in touch with you! I wanted to change the time of our tennis match and I didn't know how to reach you." My friend was shocked. Because I had faith and knew that a coincidence would occur, it did.

So go with the flow. Allow things to happen. Maintain a certain rhythm and harmony with the universe. Don't try to rush things. Get on the universe's schedule. And practice! When the phone rings, before you pick it up, say out loud who you think it is. After a while, you'll find you're always right!

Our daughter Carolyn is even better. She knows when the phone is going to ring and is great in gambling casinos.

Once, a patient of mine had an appointment with another doctor and was sitting in his office, waiting for his appointment. The doctor was running late, and the waiting room was crowded with irate people. After an hour had passed, several of them rose from their seats and left. My patient was tempted to do the same but something stopped him. All through the next hour, he kept glancing at his watch, wondering if it wouldn't be wiser, after all, for him to get up and leave. Finally, after two full hours had passed, the nurse came into the room and called out "Kirimedjian!"*

He jumped to his feet, but saw to his surprise that across the room, another man had also risen at the summons. Both men stared at each other in shock, because the name is extremely odd and unusual, and what was the likelihood of two men bearing the same uncommon name being in the same doctor's waiting room at the same time? Curious about the man's identity, my patient approached him and discovered . . . his father, whom he hadn't seen in twenty-two years! His mother had gotten divorced when he was a young child. At that time his father had been an alcoholic and abusive parent, and as a result hadn't been given any visitation rights at all. Kirimedjian grew up never knowing his father at all, to the extent that he didn't even know what he looked like,

---

* A pseudonym.

until that moment in the doctor's waiting room! Now, here's the rub: If my patient had given in to his impulse to leave, he never would have met his father! But because he allowed himself to "go with the flow" and waited, a reconciliation with his father was able to take place.

A couple of years ago, I was teaching at a college, and I wanted the students to confront the issue of their own mortality. I created an exercise where I asked them to write out their own death certificates. I instructed them to write on the certificates both their age and the cause of their deaths. I joined them in this exercise, and wrote on my certificate that I was going to die at the age of ninety-eight by falling off a ladder while working on the roof, despite my family saying I shouldn't be up there at my age doing that.

Several years later I climbed up on the roof with a pole saw to cut branches and clean gutters before we went on vacation. As I stepped off the roof, the top rung of the ladder broke off. I fell straight down and landed on my feet and fell backwards, hitting my head, but received no significant injury.

Again, I ask, how did that happen? Why didn't I get tangled in the ladder? Who or what guided or protected me and placed me safely on the ground? An overworked spirit or angel, good luck, intuition, reflex, coincidence, or God knows?

I'll leave it to you to answer. I have my experience and know the answer.

Introduction

There are moments in life when we catch our breath and glimpse God's presence. Sometimes it is when we see the radiant face of a sleeping child, sometimes it is when we hear a fragment of melody that stirs awake an unfamiliar yearning. These moments—which flicker for a tantalizing instant and then vanish in a flash—convey to us a sense of the Divine.

Every leaf, every blade of grass bears God's imprint. But these days most of us are urban dwellers leading hectic lives, and have lost the connection to the earth that enriched our forefathers and helped them see God. Obscured by skyscrapers and the haze of polluted skies, we can barely see the stars, let alone sense a Divine Presence.

Living as so many of us do lives of alienation and despair, how can we help ourselves reconnect: to God, to one another, to our very selves?

Beyond nature, there are teachers—other experiences that can help us along our journey. These guides, beacons of light and signposts in the labyrinthine wilderness in which we wander, offer us gentle instruction and compassionate encouragement as they firmly propel us back to the path from which we may have strayed.

These epiphanic experiences, common to us all, can help lead us to our unfulfilled destiny. They occur within the great universal flow of energy, and require nothing more than our sheer awareness of their presence. When consciousness is cultivated and perception is heightened, these experiences can serve as vital tokens of growth and transformation. To encounter these moments in their fullness and richness, to be aware of their message and hear their music, is truly to know God. And predominant among these experiences is the phenomenon we call *coincidences*.

Coincidences have been variously defined as "luck," "chance," "a fluke," "something out of the ordinary," or a "random conjoining of inexplicable events that defies our sense of the reasonable." We firmly believe that coincidences are much more than simple accidents or quirks of fate. To us, coincidences are blessings, the spiritual manna that hosts of angels send down to illuminate our Path. They are vivid, striking, awe-inspiring examples of Divine Providence. They are acts of God.

It has often been recounted that when the poet William Blake watched the sunrise, he would greet its arrival with an exuberant shout: "Holy! Holy! Holy!" This is how we feel when coincidences unfold in our own lives.

Thousands of years ago, God spoke to man through the sublime miracles he performed on massive and grandiose scales. In modern times we are bereft of that privilege. Today we wrestle with a hidden God, a concealed God, a God who no longer parts seas, stops the sun, or turns people into pillars of salt. Instead we have coincidences — smaller, more personal, everyday miracles. For when a coincidence does take place, it is nothing more and nothing less than God tapping us on the shoulder, whispering, or at times even shouting: "I'm here! I'm with you!"

"Coincidences," the writer Doris Lessing once said, "are God's way of remaining anonymous." *Small Miracles* attempts to strip away that facade of anonymity, and demonstrate that these seemingly random moments are instead the full and vital expressions of God's handiwork. In our own personal lives, we have been touched many times by God's radiance. In this book it is our goal to share the abundant blessings of this celestial light.

Coincidences can also be seen as opportunities for change, vital keys towards expanding our consciousness. If we can learn to become more aware of and attuned to coincidences, more cognizant of their significance, then we will evolve to a higher state of being. When we integrate both the experience and the meaning of coincidences into our lives, we open ourselves to the enriching possibilities, the blessings, and the sense of harmony with the universe that they offer.

We have written this book out of a deep sense of appreciation for God's guiding hand. Both of our fathers were Holocaust survivors whose lives were saved by inexplicable sets of uncanny coincidences. When we were children, both men independently recounted the tales of the miracles that permeated their sagas. Our respective fathers' survival was not the consequence of chance, but rather the result of divine providence. While each of these great men died over ten years ago, the message and the spiritual legacy they have imparted to us endures.

Today, both Judith and I continue to filter the inordinate number of coincidences occurring in our lives through a spiritual prism. Separately, we each embark upon a path of pursuing their deeper meaning from a spiritual perspective rather than a psychological or paranormal one. The more aware we are, we find that coincidences are constantly unfolding in our lives, sometimes at a dizzying, but certainly always exhilarating rate.

The coincidences contained in this book come from personal interviews, as well as various other sources, including newspapers, television, books, and magazines. Some are heartwarming, some awe-inspiring. Some are a nudge in a particular life-changing direction. Others demonstrate how the universe answers a question. Still others offer signs to the protagonist, a confirmation that he or she is on the right track or has done the right thing. But as much as the stories poignantly convey God's presence, they also equally impart profound teachings and precious moral lessons that can enrich our spirit and empower us to live our lives more fully. To help you along your journey, we have interpreted many of the stories, adding a few lines of commentary to reflect on their meaning and inherent value.

We hope that after reading these stories you will be able to absorb the small miracles that come into your life with an expanded mind and a different eye. As you will see, coincidences can nourish in times of hunger, enlighten in times of confusion, and comfort in times of need.

A story is told of a holy man who radiated an unusual aura of inner peace and joy. An unearthly, almost celestial glow shone from his body, and attracted vast crowds who pursued him everywhere. "Blessed one," they cried out to him, "are you a God?" "No," he answered. "Are you an angel?" "No." "Are you a prophet?" "No, I am simply awake."

We hope that *Small Miracles* will awaken you to the rich promise of a bounteous universe and the splendor lying dormant within your soul. Coincidences are everywhere and can happen any time. When your soul is ready, they will come. All that is required is that you open your heart.

Note: Names followed by an asterisk are pseudonyms.

I *don't* know if it's the hard-nosed reporter in me or the incurable romantic, but for some strange reason that I cannot fully explain, I constantly find myself poring over the "personals" in various newspapers week after week. I have been married for nineteen years and am certainly not looking for another spouse, yet I'm utterly riveted by these ads. The drama of everyday life is reflected by them, and they pay eloquent testimony to the hopes, dreams, and endurance of the human spirit.

Once in a while, I find an ad that I actually think is appropriate for a single friend of mine or for my widowed mother, and I refer them to the box number, urging that they respond. But most of the time, I just read these ads out of idle curiosity and an insatiable desire to know what lurks in romantic hearts.

One day I was scanning the personals column of a local newspaper, when I was stopped short by one particular ad. "Wow, that's unusual!" I thought. "Could this be for real?" The ad that caught my attention read: "Henrietta—do you remember we met and courted at Camp Tamiment in 1938? I've never forgotten you. Please call me. Irving . . . " and a phone number was listed, rather than the more common box I.D. "Is this some kind of joke?" I wondered aloud.

But all night long, I couldn't get the ad out of my mind. "Those personal ads cost a lot of money," I thought. "Why would someone waste so much money on a joke . . . and what's the joke here, anyway?" Finally, in the morning I couldn't take it anymore, and decided I just *had* to know the truth. Gathering my courage, I dialed the number in the ad.

As soon as the mature voice answered, I knew this was no joke, but the real thing. At that moment, I almost regretted my decision to make the call, hoping that it would not raise the elderly man's expectations, even momentarily. "Uhh . . . this is *not* Henrietta," I said quickly, "and I hope you don't mind . . . but I was so intrigued by your ad, I just had to call and find out . . . what's the story?"

Gracious and courtly in a manner that is unfortunately out of style these days, Irving amiably accommodated my inquisitiveness, and recounted the following story:

"In 1938, Henrietta and I were both counselors at Camp Tamiment, an overnight camp in Pennsylvania, and we fell in love. We were sure we were right for each other, that we'd found 'the one.' However, Henrietta's parents didn't agree. She was seventeen at the time, and they felt she was much too young to get involved in a serious relationship. So in the fall, to get her away from me, they sent her to stay with an aunt in Europe, and she lived there for several years. There she met another man, whom she married.

Heartbroken, I eventually married someone else. I never loved my wife in quite the same passionate way I loved Henrietta, but we did have a good marriage. She died three years ago, and I've been very lonely ever since. Lately, I've started to think about Henrietta a lot, and I've begun wondering if she's still alive. And if she's alive, whether she's still married. And if she's single now, could we reignite our old love? Well, you get the picture. Maybe I'm just a foolish man, but I was just hoping against hope that somehow Henrietta would see the ad. Or at least someone who knows her. I realize my chances are very slim, but I sort of thought at least I should give it a try."

I was very moved by Irving's recital, and found myself marveling at the essence of hope that resides in the human spirit, the trust and resilience that animate the soul. Irving's faith in the possibilities of the future, at the age of seventy-one, was indeed touching. I asked Irving if he would mind if I wrote a story about his search for Henrietta, and he instantly agreed, but unfortunately the editor of my magazine didn't like the idea at all. However, since I was fascinated to learn the outcome of Irving's quest and had also formed an affection for him over the phone, I kept his number and called him from time to time to see how the story played out. Sadly, he never got the phone call he was waiting for.

In 1993, two years after I first made contact with Irving, I was riding the IRT line of the New York subway system and was again engrossed in reading the personals columns of a local paper, when I heard a soft chuckle beside me. "Looking for a new husband, my dear?" the woman sitting next to me inquired with a laugh, looking pointedly at my wedding band and then at the personals page spread clearly on my lap.

"Oh," I blushed, a trifle embarrassed. "I just read them for fun. You know . . . out of curiosity. Don't you ever have the yen?" I asked her.

"Not me," she said, shaking her head adamantly, "Too much pathos in those pages. They would break my heart, those ads." She turned to me with a warm smile, "But isn't it always fascinating, the different perspectives different people have on the same things?"

My interest in her quickened. "What an intelligent woman!" I thought delightedly. "In a way, you're right," I agreed, "there *is* a lot of pathos in these pages." And I began to tell her the story of Irving's tender quest for Henrietta. She seemed mesmerized by the tale, and listened to my recital with rapt attention. "Well," I concluded at the end of my account, "I wish I could give the story a happy ending and tell you Irving found

Henrietta, but unfortunately that wasn't the case. Either Henrietta's already dead, or she lives in another city, or she just doesn't read the personals."

"It's the third choice, my dear," the woman said, patting my arm gently. "Trust me, I know."

Startled, I looked at the lined face that held vestiges of a regal beauty that had long since lost its bloom. "Do you still have his number?" she asked.

Comment

Hope is something that brings sunshine into the shadows of our lives. It is our link to a better tomorrow. When hope is gone, so too is our life force. And when hope is kept alive, so too is our determination to go on.

I was walking down a dimly lit street late one evening when I heard muffled screams coming from behind a clump of bushes. Alarmed, I slowed down to listen, and panicked when I realized that what I was hearing were the unmistakable sounds of a struggle: heavy grunting, frantic scuffling, the tearing of fabric. Only yards from where I stood, a woman was being attacked.

Should I get involved? I was frightened for my own safety, and cursed myself for having suddenly decided to take a new route home that night. What if I became another statistic? Shouldn't I just run to the nearest phone and call the police?

Although it seemed like an eternity, the deliberations in my head had taken only seconds, but already the girl's cries were growing weaker. I knew I had to act fast. How could I walk away from this? No, I finally resolved, I could not turn my back on the fate of this unknown woman, even if it meant risking my own life.

I am not a brave man, nor am I athletic. I don't know where I found the moral courage and physical strength—but once I had finally resolved to help the girl, I became strangely transformed. I ran behind the bushes and pulled the assailant off the woman. Grappling, we fell to the ground, where we wrestled for a few minutes until the attacker jumped up and escaped. Panting hard, I scrambled upright and approached the girl, who was crouched behind a tree, sobbing. In the darkness, I could barely see her outline, but I could certainly sense her trembling shock.

Not wanting to frighten her further, I at first spoke to her from a distance. "It's OK," I said soothingly. "The man ran away. You're safe now."

There was a long pause and then I heard her words, uttered in wonder, in amazement.

"Dad, is that you?"

And then, from behind the tree, stepped my youngest daughter, Katherine.

— *Greg O'Leary**

Comment:

Many people fear that their good actions will go unrewarded. How often do we hear the cynical aphorism "No good deed goes unpunished"? Yet here is a vivid example of the fact that precisely the opposite often holds true. By resolving to risk his life for an unknown woman, the father ended up saving his own daughter's life. And in his determination to help another, the father

---

* A pseudonym.

discovered the amazing force and power of the will. Under ordinary circumstances, he would have been unable to summon up the physical strength to fight off the rapist. Yet his will was so great that he drew strength from an unknown and untapped source. We have capacities of which we are not even aware. In setting out to do a good deed for another, this man did a wonderful deed for himself!

When my son Joey turned eleven, he was suddenly stricken with panic disorder, which evolved into agoraphobia. His anxiety attacks were so severe that he spent close to a year confined to his room, while my husband and I searched frantically for a cure. Finally, after eleven months of sheer hell, we found a psychiatrist who prescribed Prozac, a drug that achieved wonders. My husband and I were tremendously grateful that God had returned our son to us from the nightmare world into which he had been plunged.

During this time, we had visited a series of practitioners to determine the cause of our son's problem, and had discovered along the way that he was learning-disabled. All the years that he had been in school no one had picked up on this fact, which we were told had contributed to or even totally created the anxiety problem. Now that he was cured of panic disorder, we had to find a school that specialized in learning disabilities. This was not so easy, we soon learned to our dismay. Given his recent medical record, nobody wanted him.

All the schools that specialized in learning disabilities claimed that their students had an educational problem, not an emotional one. Our son would not fit in, they maintained; they were not equipped to handle someone like him. All the psychologists I spoke with insisted that all LD (learning-disabled) children possess emotional components as a result of their disability, but when I repeated their words to school officials my protests fell on deaf ears. He was rejected by every school we applied to.

There was one particular LD school that I really wanted to get Joey into, because it had an excellent reputation and was close to home as well. I had campaigned hard to get him into this school, but they kept turning me down. "Please give my son a chance!" I begged. But nobody wanted to, and I was growing more desperate by the minute.

One evening, I happened to attend a charity event, where I found myself seated next to an older woman named Barbara with whom I was vaguely acquainted. I knew her to be a prominent society figure, very wealthy, very influential. Suddenly, before I could think or stop myself, I found myself—to my own shock and horror— pouring out my heart to her about my continuing travails with Joey. Even as I unburdened myself to her, I felt the inappropriateness of what I was doing. "Why are you telling this woman your troubles?" I scolded myself even as I continued to describe my litany of woes. But to my own mystification and chagrin, I found I just couldn't stop. I didn't stop, in fact, until I had completely exhausted every single last detail of my struggle to get Joey into the LD school of my choice.

When I was finally finished, I was appalled at myself. What had I gone and done? But to my surprise, Barbara neither distanced herself from me nor looked at me with disdain. Instead, to my complete surprise, her eyes filled with tears, and she patted my hand consolingly, reassuringly. "Honey," she said warmly, "you've told your story to the right person! It just so happens that I live next door to the founder and director of the school, and it also just so happens that I am one of their major league contributors. In fact, I have thrown many parlor parties for this particular school and raised tremendous amounts of money. You can consider your son a new student of this school. I give you my word—you can depend on it!"

I couldn't believe my incredible luck, my great fortune! What a godsend, to have been seated next to Barbara! Sure enough, true to her word, she used her powers of persuasion and influence, and my son was accepted by the school for the coming year, where he excelled and—for the first time in his life—was placed on the honor roll.

My sense of indebtedness to Barbara was infinite, and so I kept up with her, sending gifts and cards. I called her before each holiday to wish her well, and a bond was forged between us. During this time, I learned from other people that she had experienced many problems with her own two children. The older one, a son, was a drug addict who had recently disappeared, and the younger one, a daughter, was mildly retarded and problematic in many different ways. My heart ached for Barbara, especially when she inquired, frequently, about my son's progress, and seemed genuinely delighted to learn that he was doing well.

Our relationship continued to develop for about a year — and then Barbara's husband died suddenly. I traveled to the suburbs for the funeral, where I would meet her family for the first time. As I stood on the line that slowly filed past the mourning family to offer condolences, I was suddenly struck by a familiar figure sitting beside my friend. "Who's that young woman sitting next to Barbara?" I asked the woman behind me. "Why, that's her only daughter, Nancy," she answered, "you know . . . the retarded one." I gasped, as I felt goosebumps erupt on my arms. Now everything was suddenly clear. Now I knew for certain why Barbara had been fated to be the agent of redemption for my son.

Twenty-five years before, when I had been a high school student in a private school, a mildly retarded girl whose name I had forgotten had joined our class in senior year. Although our school was not equipped for special ed cases, her wealthy parents had prevailed upon the school administration to give the girl a chance and allow her an education within a mainstream context. Their wealth and influence had overcome all objections and the girl had been admitted, albeit with great hesitation.

Life in this school, however, was not easy for this young woman. She was viewed as both an outcast and a pariah. She was cruelly shunned by virtually everyone — everyone that is, except me. I had always championed the underdog. I had great sympathy for those on the fringe, and had always made an effort to reach out to them — as I reached out to this girl.

On our high school graduation trip to Washington, D.C., no one wanted to room with her in the hotel. I volunteered, and although the experience wasn't an easy one, I was glad that I had done so. After graduation, the class dispersed and separated, striking out in different directions. Some I hadn't ever seen again, some I had forgotten about. Like . . . Nancy.

For it was Nancy who was the young woman sitting next to Barbara. It was Nancy, long-lost, long-forgotten Nancy, who was in fact Barbara's daughter. During our senior year together, I had never met nor spoken with Nancy's mother, and we had never had occasion to be introduced. Yet our lives had apparently become inextricably connected, our destinies fated to intersect. As the line slowly worked its way towards the mourners, and I drew closer to Barbara and Nancy to pay my respects, my eyes filled with tears.

Twenty-five years ago, I had helped Barbara's daughter. Twenty-five years later, Barbara had repaid the favor and helped me with my son.

Perhaps our own memories are sadly too short, but happily God's is blessedly long.

— *Blanche Purcell**

Comment

When we perform a charitable deed or benevolent action, it doesn't disappear into a vacuum or a spiritual black hole; ultimately we can expect to be repaid. Sometimes, we are repaid within a matter of moments or hours after executing the kindness, and can immediately see the connection between our deed and our reward. However, there are deeds that take decades to be repaid, but when they finally are, we often gasp at their fitting symmetry! Of course, virtue is its own reward and the desire for compensation is rarely the reason we perform acts of kindness. Nonetheless, it is heartening to receive a nod of acknowledgment from God every now and then, an affirmation that we did the right thing and that our deeds are duly registered with a universe that remembers.

*F*or fifty-two years, Robert Adkins thought his best friend, Roy Stump, was dead. After all, hadn't he cradled his dying friend's head in his lap and then watched a medic remove his dog tags?

"Everyone in the platoon was sure Roy was dead," Robert recalled one day in April 1996 as he chatted with a stranger in a waiting room at Lorain Community/St. Joseph Regional Health Center in Lorain, Ohio. Robert was waiting for his wife, Juanita, to return from cataract surgery. The stranger was waiting for his brother-in-law, also in surgery. Somehow, the conversation turned to World War II.

"We were stationed in Holland and were watching a buddy defuse an anti-tank mine when it blew up," Adkins said. The man working on the mine was killed, and shrapnel struck Stump in the head, chest, and other parts of his body. The worst injury was the gaping head wound that Adkins tried to tend by applying pressure with his handkerchief, unmindful of a smaller wound in his own forehead.

As they continued to talk, Robert, now seventy-two years old, was astonished to learn that the stranger, like him, had served in the 787th Anti-Aircraft Battalion in 1944. Skeptical about the coincidence, they began grilling each other, as if in a test.

"Who was the platoon sergeant?" Robert asked the stranger.

The man answered correctly. "Was anyone killed in that battalion?" he shot back.

"I just told you, my best buddy, Roy D. Stump," Robert replied.

The man smiled and said, "I hate to disappoint you, but I am very much alive."

Robert sat stunned. "I thought he was going to have a heart attack," Stump remembered. "I hadn't recognized him at first, but I knew who he was as soon as he said his nickname was 'Sloop.' Mine was 'Little Red.' I had bright red hair then," said Stump, stroking his gray crewcut.

To prove his identity, the seventy-one-year-old Stump produced a faded copy of his discharge papers and a driver's license with his name on it. Then the two men hugged and "everybody in the waiting room thought we were crazy," Robert said.

Stump had been critically injured, but he hadn't died as the other platoon members had believed. An emergency operation in a field tent had saved his life, and he had been transferred to a hospital in Belgium, where he remained for eighteen months, recovering from forty-two wounds, including one that left him with a metal plate in his head.

By the time he got out of the hospital, the war was over and he had no idea where the rest of the platoon members were living. He often wondered what had happened to his buddy, Sloop.

He always credited his friend—along with an Army-issue combination Bible, almanac, and dictionary and a leather wallet he carried in his breast pocket—with saving his life. Shrapnel had torn through the wallet and Bible into his chest but had missed his heart.

In an odd twist of fate, both men moved to Lorain, Ohio, after the war and raised families there. For more than forty years, they lived only a few miles apart and never knew it. "I probably drove by his house three or four times a week and didn't even know he lived there," Roy Stump said.

The men have had no difficulty in picking up their friendship where it left off. The night after their chance meeting, they had dinner with their wives, and later that week they went to the speedway together. And, like the kids they were forty-two years ago, they exchanged pocket knives.

Carol Anderson was a young widow whose husband had died of cancer at thirty-five. Bob Edwards was a young widower whose wife had been killed in a car accident at twenty-nine. Both marriages had been extremely happy, and both Carol and Bob were sure they would never love or marry again. After many lonely years of pain and suffering, they met at a church dinner and started courting. When they got engaged and then married, they told everyone "it was miraculous that they had found each other." Their relationship was strong and loving. The only trouble spot in the marriage was that they had diametrically different opinions on what to do about the past.

Carol longed to bury it; Bob needed to explore it. Carol never wanted to talk about either of their previous marriages. Bob, on the other hand, was eager to know the most minute details of Carol's life before they had met, and was hurt that Carol showed such a complete lack of interest in his. "Why raise ghosts?" Carol would ask when Bob would persist with his gentle probings and soft inquiries. "Memory should be preserved, not obliterated," he would reply. This went on for years, with Carol's perspective ultimately prevailing. As a result, they never shared stories, pictures, or mementos from their first marriages.

Ten years later, Carol felt that their marriage was secure enough to withstand any assaults from the past. "Okay," she told Bob one day, "I'm ready to talk." She began telling Bob about her first marriage and pulled out several snapshot albums she had hidden from him all these years. "These are from our honeymoon," she said, starting to leaf through the pages of one album. "We went to France. Oh . . . here we are at Lourdes."

"You went to Lourdes?" Bob said with mild interest. "So did we."

"Well, I guess half the world goes to Lourdes," Carol laughed, "no big deal. Everyone's looking for blessings and miracles in their lives."

"Wait a second, Carol, turn back a page," said Bob suddenly. "Let me see that snapshot again of you and Ralph at Lourdes." Carol obligingly turned back the page.

"Carol," her husband asked tensely, "Who's that couple in the background?"

"I have no idea," she said. "Just as the photographer snapped the picture, a couple walked by and got caught by the shutter. I can see why you asked, though, thinking they were with us. In the picture, it does look as though they're standing behind us, almost as if they're posing, but it's just an illusion.

"You're wrong, Carol," Bob said slowly, "it wasn't a mistake, it was destiny. You see . . . that couple in the background . . . is me and my first wife."

Comment

Millions of people travel to Lourdes each year. What were the chances of Carol and Bob not only being at the same place at the same time but also "coincidentally" appearing together in a photo at the holy shrine? When the picture was taken, they lived in different parts of the United States, and were not members of the same association, organization, or tour group. They were not connected to each other in any way—except in God's plan. The people who make pilgrimages to Lourdes are more often than not the ill, the infirm, and the elderly, rather than young people like Carol and Bob. Life had just begun for each couple, and seemingly neither Bob nor Carol needed a miracle. But they did . . . only they hadn't known it at the time.

*A*s a young bride in the summer of 1972, Faith Peterson* came to the Adirondack cottage of her in-laws for a visit. Her doting husband, Kevin, took her rowing in an idyllic lake framed by pastoral woods. In the boat, sighing contentedly, Faith languidly swished her fingers through the cool water, enjoying the bracing feel of the wet cold against her warm hand.

Curling up in a corner of the boat and half-dozing, Faith continued running her hand through the water until she suddenly became aware that her diamond engagement ring had slipped off her finger. "Oh my God!" she shrieked to her husband as she sat bolt upright in the boat. "My ring's gone! It must have fallen into the water!"

"That's impossible," Kevin said with skepticism. "You probably left it in a drawer at the cottage."

"No," she insisted, "I never take it off, never. And besides . . . just as we were about to climb into the boat, a woman at the dock complimented me on it. So I know I had it on."

"But how could it have fallen off your finger, Faith?"

"My hand was in the water, Kevin, and the ring was a little loose to begin with. It must have just slipped off . . . "

"Okay, don't worry, I'll find it," Kevin reassured her, and dove into the shallow lake to begin searching the bottom.

All day long, he dove again and again into the crystalline waters of the placid lake, confident he would successfully ferret out the missing ring. After all, there was no powerful current coursing through the lake that could have carried the ring away, and there was little debris below the surface that could have trapped it. But each time that his head bobbed to the surface, the story was the same. "Not yet!" he would yell bravely to Faith as she sat forlornly in the boat, peering anxiously at him. "I'll find it this time for sure!" he would smile valiantly, descending into the water for yet another foray.

Finally, at nightfall, Kevin called it quits. "I'm so sorry, honey," he said to his disconsolate spouse, putting an arm around her shoulder. "I tried my best."

"I know you did, Kevin."

"And it's not as if the ring isn't insured. We'll get you another one."

"Kevin, you're sweet and I know you mean well, but another ring just won't be the same. This is the diamond you gave me when you proposed, when we pledged our eternal love. I treasured it as a symbol, for its meaning and sentimental value. Any other diamond will just be an expensive rock. No, it's the original ring I want," Faith said stubbornly. "If I can't have the one I lost, then I don't want another. Let's use the insurance money for something practical, like furniture."

"Okay, honey," Kevin shrugged, too drained from the day's rigors to argue. So Faith never got a substitute—not even when they were wealthy and could easily afford one.

In 1992, when Faith and Kevin were a middle-aged couple with teenage children of their own, they took their family to the same Adirondack cottage where they had vacationed as newlyweds. Kevin had inherited it from his parents when they had died, but had since that first visit never returned to the cottage, preferring to rent it out instead. For years, they had sent their children to overnight camp, but this summer the kids had rebelled. "C'mon, Dad," they argued, "we're too old for camp. Let's go to the Adirondacks for the summer and use Gramps's cottage."

When they arrived at the cottage, Kevin was excited. "Let me take you out to the lake," he said to his kids as his wife was unpacking. "You don't mind, do you, hon?"

"No, go ahead, enjoy yourselves! It's actually much easier for me to finish when you're all out of the way," Faith said, laughing.

"Hey, Dad, can I take my fishing rod along?" asked the youngest.

"Sure, I hear the fish are really biting today."

When they returned home a few hours later, Kevin and the kids proudly held aloft their prize catch of the day: a huge trout that weighed in at seven pounds. "Guess what's for dinner?" Kevin winked at Faith, as she directed the requisite "oohs" and "aahs" at her youngest, who was glowing with unmasked pride. "I never caught such a big one before," he said.

"It sure is a great catch," Faith agreed, as she placed the trout on a cutting board and slit it open with a knife.

"It sure *is* a great catch," she repeated, staring in shock at the entrails of the fish. With a sweeping motion of her hand, she beckoned her husband to her side.

Inside the belly of the trout was Faith's diamond ring.

Comment
When you cherish the emotional value of a gift, it can never really be lost, for what you carry in your heart is yours to keep, forever.

Every Sunday morning, at exactly 9 A.M., the twenty members of a church choir would assemble in the chapel of their small Southern Baptist congregation for a one-hour rehearsal before services. The choir consisted of long-time members who were dedicated, enthusiastic, and extremely punctual.

One Sunday morning, the tranquil air of the sleepy Southern town was suddenly pierced by a loud blast. Residents rushed outdoors to see what was happening, and then watched in anguish as flames spurted out the windows of the small church. They checked the time, glancing at their watches, the clocks on their kitchen walls, the alarms on the night tables in their bedrooms. It was ten minutes past nine.

Gasps, wails, and shrieks filled the air as the townspeople raced towards the church. The volunteer firemen who had preceded them by a few minutes shook their heads mournfully as they arrived. In just seconds, the church had been totally consumed by flames. "It probably was a gas explosion," one of the firemen said. "It happened too fast. None of the choir members could have gotten out in time. I'm sorry. It doesn't look like there are any survivors at all."

Everyone reacted differently. Some people bowed their heads and turned away in silence, griefstricken. A few women crumpled onto the charred grass. Others collapsed into one another's arms and emitted heartrending sobs. Paralyzed by shock, people didn't seem to notice the sudden convergence of twenty automobiles pulling into the church's parking lot at the same time. No one seemed to observe the twenty red-frocked figures running towards the church.

"Hey, what happened?" they heard a familiar-sounding alto voice inquire, shattering the silence that had fallen over the mourners.

"Yeah, what's going on?" chimed in another well-known voice, a mellifluous soprano. "My God, the church is in ruins!" shouted an unforgettable baritone. In wonder, astonishment, and dazed disbelief, the townspeople gazed at the miraculous sight of all twenty choir members—vital and alive—streaming in their direction.

For the first time in twelve years of ongoing choir practice, every single one of them—for separate, different, and unconnected reasons—had come late.

he dinette set was in a sorry state of disrepair. Pressed into service as props for such childhood games as musical chairs and Fort Apache, it was badly battered—a mere shadow of the gleaming chrome set that had once graced our kitchen. Stuffing was spilling out of the seat cushions. It had become a real eyesore, and I felt embarrassed each time a visitor entered my home.

In February 1996, I came into a little money and decided to splurge on a new dinette set. I scouted the neighborhood stores that had been recommended by savvy friends, and finally found a set that made my heart sing. I fell in love with its smooth, sleek, contemporary look, the clean, sharp angles of its matching chairs, and its black and white Formica finish. For me, buying a dinette set was a virtual event, and I felt thrilled that I had encountered one that I liked so much. I was, however, less than thrilled to learn its price tag: $680, more than the budget I had allotted in my head. "You have great taste!" the storeowner congratulated me. "You've chosen one of the most popular models we sell." I sighed. Story of my life: champagne taste on a beer budget! I really didn't want to spend that much money, but this set really tempted me. I stood undecided in the store, until finally the practical side of me took charge, and I regretfully told the storeowner, "Sorry, but I just can't spend that much. Thanks again." As I departed the store, I threw one final, yearning look at the dinette set of my dreams.

The next week, I called a friend renowned for extraordinary bargain-hunting abilities, and she gave me a list of dinette outlets in the neighborhood that sold cheaper models. Armed with the list, I left my home to make the rounds once again.

The day dawned gray and overcast—the kind of day that invariably makes your spirits sag and diminishes your enthusiasm, even for bargain hunting. Nonetheless, I was determined to follow my agenda, so I drove to the first outlet store on my list. Somehow, my friend had made a mistake: all the sets there were priced well over a thousand dollars, and mumbling embarrassed thanks to the storeowner, I beat a hasty retreat. By this time it was raining hard, and I ran to my car, parked a block away.

It was then that I saw her. An elderly woman, shuffling slowly in the torrential downpour, clad only in a thin cotton dress and sneakers, with no umbrella, raincoat, or rain hat to protect her from the slashing rain. She looked pale, wan, and vulnerable. She also looked vaguely familiar, and I broke off my wild dash to the car to approach her. As I advanced closer, I made the connection: She was an impoverished woman whom a charitable organization sent every year to the dress shop I owned for donations of clothing. I had an agreement with this organization whereby I gave, through their referral, free clothing to the neighborhood's poor. She came regularly, once a year, to be outfitted, but I had never seen her outside the store before.

"Linda," I asked in concern, "why are you out on a morning like this?" She began to sob. "Let me drive you to your destination," I said, propelling her to my car.

"What's the matter?" I asked inside the car, as she began to wail in an almost unearthly manner. She poured out her tale of woe and I felt stricken by her story. She had a daughter who was retarded and married to a retarded man. Unexpectedly, they had been able to carve out a happy life for themselves and had two normal children. Unfortunately, however, due to their disabilities, they were unable to make a living to sustain their modest lifestyle. Here and there they got odd jobs occasionally and some minimal government assistance, but not enough to live on. The husband's parents were dead, and Linda herself was on welfare. Unable to pay the rent, her daughter had received an eviction notice, and her daughter's landlord had warned her that if he didn't receive the overdue amount by today, she and her family would be ejected from the premises with nowhere to go.

I had three hundred dollars in my wallet. As Linda cried pitifully in my car, I pulled out a hundred-dollar bill and handed it to her. She stared at the bill in astonishment, kissed me, thanked me effusively, but continued to cry. I paused for a moment, then pulled out a second hundred-dollar bill and handed it to her. She acknowledged her fervent gratitude a second time, but her tears still flowed unabated. I hesitated the third time, but thought, "Aw, what the heck? What's a dinette set compared to the eviction of a family?" and handed her the final hundred-dollar bill. Then I drove her to the office of the charitable organization from which she hoped to solicit further help, and kissed her goodbye.

As I drove away, I was in a positive frame of mind, confident that I had done the right thing. I was proud that I had made the sacrifice. But as I neared my destination—the second dinette outlet store on my list— I began to waver, assaulted by conflicting emotions. Maybe I was a fool, a patsy, an easy touch. Maybe I should have just given her a hundred? Maybe the charitable organization—funded by individuals certainly wealthier than I—could have undertaken the full cost of the rent, and my sacrifice had been needless. By the time I reached the dinette store, I was no longer sure that my three-hundred-dollar donation had been necessary or even justified.

But as soon as I entered the dinette store, my anxiety about the money dissipated, as my attention was drawn to the dinette set of my dreams—the exact same set I had fallen in love with the week before—standing in the center of the showroom. "Excuse me," I excitedly asked the salesman who approached me, "how much is that set over there—the white one with the black formica trim?"

"Oh, that one!" he said. "You sure have great taste—it's beautiful, isn't it?"

"So how much is it?" I asked with mounting excitement. "Well," he said slowly, "it really *is* an expensive set, but you know . . . it's going to be discontinued soon so I don't mind giving you the floor sample. It's ordinarily much more money, but I'll give it to you for . . . three hundred eighty dollars!" Exactly three hundred dollars less than the original set I had seen the week before.

For a fraction of a second, I closed my eyes to thank God for his blessing on my charity and also . . . for the dinette set!

— *Yitta Halberstam Mandelbaum*

Comment

To the extent that we give to others, the universe responds in kind.

That year, winter in New York City lingered lazily into late April. Living alone and legally blind, I had tended to remain indoors much of the time.

Finally, one day, the chill was gone and spring stepped forth, filling the air with a penetrating and exhilarating fragrance. Outside my backyard window, a merry little bird kept chirping persistently, beckoning me, it seemed, outdoors.

Aware of the capriciousness of April, I clung to my winter coat, but, as a concession to the change in temperature, discarded my woolen scarf, hat, and gloves. Taking my three-pronged cane, I stepped out cheerfully onto my open porch leading directly to the sidewalk. Lifting my face to the sun, I gave it a welcoming smile in acknowledgment of its warmth and promise.

As I walked down my quiet dead-end street, my next door neighbor called out a musical "Hello" and asked if I wanted a lift to where I was going. "No, thank you," I called back in return. "These legs of mine have been resting all winter, and my joints are badly in need of an outing, so I think I'll walk."

Reaching the corner, I waited, as was my habit, for someone to come along who would let me walk across with them when the light turned green. It seemed to take somewhat longer than usual for the sound of traffic to cease, yet I had no offers. As I stood there patiently, I began to hum a tune that returned to me from somewhere in the back of my head. It was a "welcome to spring" song I had learned in school as a child.

Suddenly, a strong, well-modulated masculine voice spoke up. "You sound like a very cheerful human being," it said. "May I have the pleasure of your company across the street?" Flattered by such chivalry, I nodded, smiling, whispering a barely audible "Yes."

Gently, he tucked his hand around my upper arm and together we stepped off the curb. As we slowly made our way across, we talked of the most obvious topic—the weather—and about how good it was to be alive on such a day. As we kept in step together, it was difficult to determine who was the guide and who was the one being led.

We had barely reached the other side of the crossing, when horns impatiently began blasting forth again at what was assuredly a change in the light. We walked on a few more paces to get away from the curb. Turning to him, I opened my mouth to thank him for his assistance and company. Before a single word had left my lips, he spoke up. "I don't know if you realize," he said, "how gratifying it is to find someone as cheerful as you to accompany a blind person like me across the street."

That spring day has stayed with me forever.

— *Charlotte Wechsler*

Comment

Sometimes, when we feel most alone in the universe, God sends us a "twin"—a mirror image—to buffer and assuage our sense of differentness and isolation.

*H*e was born to a life of privilege and — as the times mandated — rebelled fiercely when he was nineteen. Donning the faded, torn denim uniform of his generation, Joey Riklis* dropped out of college, quit his part-time job, and announced to his widowed father that he was taking off for India in search of "enlightenment." Sensitive and psychologically astute, his father, Adam Riklis, withstood this blow with equanimity and grace, heeding the advice of friends who counseled patience, tolerance, and love. Joey was acting "normal for his age," they explained confidently, and the storm would soon blow over, they were sure. So Adam told his son that he understood that he was testing his wings and carving out his own unique identity, and he assured him that he accepted the convulsions erupting in his life with sympathy and understanding. But when Joey revealed one day that he had broken with his religion, his father snapped.

Adam Riklis was a Holocaust survivor. His entire family had been murdered by the Nazis, and he alone had withstood the barbaric hardships of three concentration camps. Upon learning that he was the sole survivor of his family, he had silently pledged that the religion his relatives had died for would not die with him. Although many survivors had come away with the opposite attitude, abandoning the religion of their youth in anger and pain, Adam's perspective had been quite different. To divorce himself from the religion of his murdered relatives would be no less than a betrayal of their lives . . . and deaths.

In Cleveland, Adam had clung tightly to his Jewish traditions and religious rituals, carefully incorporating them into his family's day-to-day existence. He sent his children to Hebrew day school, took them to synagogue regularly, and saw to it that they adhered strictly to religious law. He was proud that he had raised religious children who would carry on the family's heritage. But now his own son was announcing that he was scorning this very legacy, making a mockery of his family's losses. Adam could countenance anything but this.

"Get out of here!" he screamed at Joey. "Get out of my home and never come back! You are not my son. I disown you from my heart, from my soul, from my life. I never want to see you again!"

"Well, that's just fine with me," Joey shouted back, "because I never want to see you again either!"

In India, Joey traveled from guru to guru, seeking wisdom, spirituality—concrete answers to life's elusive mysteries. During his travels, he hooked up with Sarah, his female counterpart in many ways. She too had dropped out of a religious Jewish home and was looking for another spiritual path. They were certain they were "soul mates." They had been together for six years when Joey accidentally encountered an old classmate from Cleveland on a street corner in Bombay.

Joey and Sammy embraced happily. "This is unbelievable!" they told each other. They were avidly trading the stories of their respective adventures when Sammy's eyes clouded and he said somberly, "Hey, Joey, I was really sorry to hear about your dad."

"My dad?" Joey repeated dumbly. "What do you mean?"

"Oh my God, I'm so sorry. Then you don't know, obviously."

"Know what?" Joey asked, now rigid with dread.

"Oh, Joey, your father died a couple of months ago. No one wrote you?"

"No one knew where I was," Joey replied slowly, dumbstruck by the news. "What did he die of?"

"A heart attack."

"Not a heart attack," Joey said, his eyes welling with tears. "More like a broken heart, I'm sure. And I'm the cause. I killed him. I killed my own father."

"Joey, don't be ridiculous," Sarah murmured, touching his shoulder in compassion. "You had nothing to do with your father's death!"

"Sarah, you're wrong," Joey answered. "I had *everything* to do with my father's death!"

For several days afterward, Joey lived in a stupor, dazed with grief and remorse. He could not shake his overwhelming certainty that the pain he had inflicted on his father had taken his life. In the back of his mind, he had always hoped for a reconciliation. Somehow he had been sure that a loving reunion would one day take place. Now he would never be able to ask his father's forgiveness, or return to the warm embrace of his love. And he would never have the closure, the resolution, that he so desperately needed.

"Sarah," he shook his head mournfully a few days after learning of his father's death. "I can't go on like this anymore. India tastes like ashes to me now. I know you'll think I'm strange but I have to go . . . to Israel."

"Israel!" Sarah said in surprise, wrinkling her nose in distaste as only an entrenched religious rebel could. "Why do you want to go to Israel?"

"I just feel a pull, Sarah. I can't explain it, but I have to go."

"Okay, okay, so we'll go," she agreed unhappily.

When the plane landed, Joey turned to Sarah and said, "I want to go pray."

"Are you turning weird on me, Joey?" she asked in mock concern.

"Sarah, please!"

"Okay, okay," she relented, "so you want to pray, fine. You want to go to a synagogue?"

"No, Sarah, I want to go to the Wall. It's the only remnant left of the First and Second Temples — considered the holiest site in Jerusalem. People believe that God's presence is stronger there than in any other place in Israel. It's where people from all over the world go to pray, to petition God, to ask for miracles. What I want to do is pray for my father's forgiveness."

"Okay," Sarah said, "let's go. But I have to tell you I don't like the direction you seem to be taking."

"Sarah!" Joey cried out in anguish. "Why don't you understand?"

"I understand only too well, Joey. I understand that you're not the same Joey I knew all these years. You used to laugh at all this crap together with me. And now you want to go pray at a wall."

"Look, Sarah, I'm in pain. I loved my father. He's dead. I feel I killed him. Why are you making this so hard for me?"

They quarreled for an hour, and finally decided to split up. "Sarah, I don't know why this is happening," Joey said sadly. "I thought you were my soul mate."

"I am," she said softly, planting a tender and regretful kiss on his cheek. "But our souls simply aren't in alignment anymore. Goodbye, Joey."

Approaching the Wall on foot, Joey looked from a distance at the clusters of people thronging the plaza. Ethiopians in African headdress, Yemenites in white traditional robes, Americans in T-shirts and little yarmulkes. All coming to press their lips against the cool stones, cry warm tears, and fervently beseech God with their personal petitions.

Joey approached a security guard, one of dozens tensely scanning the crowds. "Excuse me," he said. "Can I get a prayer book anywhere around here?"

Silently, the guard pointed in the direction of a bearded rabbi, who was dispensing religious paraphernalia—yarmulkes, prayer books, women's scarves—to the uninitiated.

Donning a borrowed yarmulke and clutching a prayer book, Joey made his way to a section of the Wall. Watching the others and simulating their movements, he rested his head against the smooth stone of the Wall, tried to encircle it with his arm to create an aura of privacy, and began to silently pray. He thought the words would seem foreign after all these years and that he would chant them haltingly, but instead they flowed forth from him in a familiar, comforting stream. He closed his eyes and recalled his father's intonation of these same words, as he was transported back in memory to different realms, the world of his youth. "Oh, Dad," he sobbed. "How I wish I could ask your forgiveness! How I wish I could tell you how much I loved you! How much I regret all the pain I caused you! I didn't mean to hurt you, Dad. I was just trying to find my own way. You meant everything to me, Dad. I wish I could tell you that."

When Joey finished praying, he turned around, at a loss at what to do next. Then he observed people around him scribbling notes and inserting them into the crevices of the Wall. Curious as to what this behavior meant, he approached a young man, and asked, "Excuse me, why are so many people putting little pieces of paper into the cracks of the Wall?"

"Oh, these are their petitions," the youth answered, "their prayers. It is believed that the stones are so holy that requests placed inside of them will be especially blessed."

"Can I do that, too?" Joey asked, intrigued.

"Sure. But be warned, it isn't easy to find an empty crevice anymore!" the young man laughed. "Jews have been coming here for centuries to ply God with their prayers!"

Joey wrote: "Dear Father, I beg you to forgive me for the pain I caused you. I loved you very much and I will never forget you. And please know that nothing that you taught me was in vain. I will not betray your family's deaths. I promise."

When he had finished writing the note, Joey searched for a empty crevice. The young man had not exaggerated. All of the Wall's cracks were filled, crammed, overflowing with petitioners' notes, and it took him close to an hour to find an empty space. But it turned out not to be empty, after all. When he slid his own small note into the crack, he accidentally dislodged another that had already been resting there, and it fell to the ground. "Oh, no, I've pushed out someone's note," Joey thought, a little panic-stricken, wondering what he should do with it. He stooped down to retrieve it, and holding the rolled-up paper in his palm, began searching for another space in which to insert it. But suddenly overcome by a tremendous curiosity to read the words of the unknown petitioner, Joey did something uncharacteristically unscrupulous: He rolled open the note to examine its contents. And this is what he read:

"My Dear Son Joey, If you should ever happen to come to Israel and somehow miraculously find this note, this is what I want you to know: I always loved you, even when you hurt me, and I will never stop loving you. You are, and always will be, my beloved son. And Joey, please know that I forgive you for everything, and only hope that you in turn will forgive a foolish old man." The note was signed "Adam Riklis, Cleveland, Ohio."

"Sir, are you all right, Sir . . . Sir . . . ?" The disembodied voice came from a distance, shattering Joey's reverie. He didn't know how long he had been standing there, numb, paralyzed with shock, clutching his father's note in his trembling hand, tears flowing in rivulets down his face. Stunned, he turned to face the young man who had instructed him on the writing of the petition minutes ago. "Listen," said the young man warmly, draping a sympathetic arm around Joey's shoulder, "you don't have to tell me. It will be Sabbath soon, it's almost sundown. Would you like to come spend it with me?"

Three years later, Joey had returned to his religion and was a full-time rabbinical student. "I think it's time for you to marry," the head rabbi said to him one day. "My wife likes to play matchmaker and she says she has the perfect girl for you. I've told her about you, and she says she's positive she has found your soul mate. It's someone like yourself—a returnee to Judaism—who studies at my wife's women's school. Would you like to meet her? Come to my house tonight for dinner, and she'll be there."

That evening, Joey entered the rabbi's house and was escorted to the living room. There, sitting on the couch, was none other than his old love, Sarah. They stared across the room at each other in shock and awe, and Sarah blinked back tears. "How . . . how did this happen, Sarah?" Joey asked in stunned surprise.

"Well, after we split up," Sarah said, "I began to wander around Israel. 'I'm here already, I might as well see the country before I head back to India,' I told myself. So I started trekking around, and despite myself began to fall in love with the country, the people, and . . .

the religion. One day, someone told me about a great women's school, so here I am!"

"Sarah, I thought about you so often all these years . . . "

"Well, I guess our souls are in alignment now," she said softly, as she turned to him with a welcoming smile.

Smoke poured out from under the front hood of the black stretch limousine as it sped down the highway. Louis, the limousine's chauffeur, pulled over to the side of the road to flag down assistance. Concern and worry were written on his face. He stood in the cold rain and frantically waved a flashlight in the air, hoping to draw people to his plight. It was futile. Most drivers slowed down to catch a glimpse of the stalled limousine, but then blithely continued on their way.

Robert Wise* was the exception. He noted the chauffeur's predicament and felt compelled to come to his aid. He drove up to the shoulder of the road, peered out his window, and asked how he could help. "Would you please call my boss and tell him my situation?" asked the chauffeur. "And then could you please let me know what he says?"

"No problem," came the cheerful reply. Louis then provided Robert with the name of his boss, Mr. Cavendish*, and a phone number. Robert got back on the highway, drove to the nearest service station, and made the call.

A short time later, Robert returned. He relayed a message from Mr. Cavendish and then turned on his engine, ready to continue on his way home. "Wait!" Louis called out to him. "How can I thank you?"

"Oh, please, it was nothing," replied Robert.

"No, you must tell me how I can thank you," the chauffeur insisted.

"It was really nothing," came the reply, "but if you care to, you can send a dozen roses to my wife for her birthday, which is next week." Robert gave Louis his address, and the two men departed.

The following day, the chauffeur told his boss what had happened on the road. He described how difficult it had been to get assistance and how glad he had been when a kind stranger finally stopped to help. "And all the man asked for were flowers for his wife," concluded the chauffeur. Mr. Cavendish listened and was touched by Robert's modest request. He took the address and said, "Leave the rest to me."

Within the next few weeks, Mr. Cavendish arranged for flowers to be sent to the Wise home. But that was not all. For years, the couple had been struggling financially and were threatened with foreclosure. They were now blessed with a generosity of spirit. In addition to the dozen red roses, Mr. Cavendish graciously paid off the mortgage on their house.

*A*t Sullivan County Community College, the students began filing in for the summer program. "Hey, look who's there," one girl said, pointing to a tall young man with curly dark hair. "It's Eddy."

"That's odd," her friend responded. "I thought Eddy had transferred to Nassau Community College on Long Island. Guess I was wrong." The two young women waved at the person they thought was Eddy. It was actually someone named Robert Shafran and this was his first day at a new college.

Moments later, a fellow running to class spotted Robert from the corner of his eye. "Hey buddy," he called out to Robert, "glad to see you. Catch you later," and he rushed by. Robert was taken aback. He knew he had never seen this person before and yet he had been greeted as if the two were on intimate terms. Just as Robert was mulling this over in his mind, an attractive young woman gave him a kiss that obviously meant more than hello.

Robert was perplexed. He had never been the recipient of such an outpouring of warmth. He was bewildered and he hoped he wasn't dreaming. Robert walked into his first class, took a seat, and settled in. No sooner had he taken a notebook out of his briefcase when a total stranger walked up to him demanding an apology. "But for what?" asked Robert, dumbfounded. "I don't even know you."

"What do you mean, you don't know me?" said the stranger. "What a sense of humor!" he chuckled.

Robert was startled and said, "Hey, I'm not who you think I am." The stranger threw Robert a quizzical look, then muttered something under his breath and walked off.

These encounters continued to happen throughout the day as Robert walked around on campus. Meanwhile a student named Michael Dominitz had heard that his best friend's lookalike had been seen on campus. Michael searched all over and then gasped when he finally spotted Robert in the distance. Indeed, there was an uncanny resemblance to Eddy Galland, his close buddy. Michael walked up to Robert and exclaimed, "Why, you're a carbon copy of my best friend!" Then he pulled out a photo from his wallet. "Here, look at this," he said pointing to a picture of Eddy, "tell me what you think." Now it was Robert's turn to stand in awe as he looked at what appeared to be a picture of himself. He was astounded, just as everyone else who had made the mistake that day. "When is your birthday?" inquired Michael.

"July 12, 1961," replied Robert.

"Oh, my God," said Michael, "That's the same day as Eddy's birthday." Michael was tentative about inquiring further, but he did so despite himself. "I know Eddy was adopted. Were you adopted?"

"Yes," said Robert, incredulous as the moment unfolded.

A few days later, Michael called Eddy at his home in New Hyde Park, Long Island, and put him in touch with his lookalike. Over the phone they exchanged vital statistics and without any hesitation agreed to meet in person. "I'll drive you out there," offered Michael, who knew the way to Eddy's house and was eager to see the outcome of this exchange.

The following day, the two met, and were stunned to discover that they were virtual "doubles." Fascinated and mystified by the striking resemblance, they had an excited conversation and discovered a number of amazing similarities. They talked alike and had identical birthmarks. They both smoked too many Marlboros, and even held their cigarettes the same way. They had the same I.Q. of 148. They favored Italian food and had the same taste in music and sports. Both had a preference for dating older women.

"Isn't this bizarre?" said Robert.

"Yes, you're my clone!" said Eddy.

Both Robert and Eddy had known that they had been adopted but had been unaware that they had any siblings. Calls were made to their respective parents and the records of Long Island Jewish Hospital were checked. That which they had sensed from the moment they had made contact was now confirmed. Eddy and Robert were twins, separated at birth.

The story hit the news and the picture of the reunited brothers appeared on the front page of newspapers everywhere. The story made for good conversation — another interesting bit of news, quickly absorbed, rapidly forgotten.

Forgotten by everyone, that is, except for one young man named David Kellman, a freshman at New York's Queens College. He called the Galland household and without skirting the issue, got right to the point. "You're not going to believe this," he said to Eddy, "but my name is David Kellman and I'm looking in the mirror and at the picture in the paper. I believe I'm the third brother." Eddy's jaw dropped open and he sat for ten minutes in total awe. "I can't believe it," were the only words that he was able to articulate.

When David arrived at the Galland residence in Long Island, Eddy opened the door and looked at him, then closed the door and then opened it again and looked and then closed it again. When he finally let David in the door, they both exclaimed "Holy cow," in unison, and stared at each other in stunned amazement. "I always knew I was adopted but I had no idea that I had any siblings," said David.

"Neither did I," said Eddy, "neither did I." They talked, they laughed, and they cried.

The records at Manhattan's Louise Wise adoption agency made it all credible. Robert, David, and Eddy were triplets, born in that order, within twenty-seven minutes of each other.

The families got together in celebration. Reporters were there to cover the story. "Looking around at the sea of new faces, what can you tell us about your new family?" asked an interviewer.

Eddy spoke up. "It's like I've known them all my life," he said, "I think the whole thing is beautiful."

Pictures were taken as David, Eddy, and Robert slung their arms around one another, each flashing a broad grin. The triplets, separated at birth, were reunited.

They went on to establish the well-known Triplets Romanian Steakhouse, located in Manhattan, which still exists today.

Comment
Bloodlines may run so deep as to pierce through all barriers that threaten to stand in their way.

he ad in the paper caught my attention immediately. "Director of Programming sought for women's organization to create and coordinate conferences, symposiums, book and author luncheons, etc.," it read. "Knowledge of current affairs and contemporary literature necessary. Experience required." My heart began to thump with excitement. "Yes!" I thought with growing elation. "This is it! This is the job I've been seeking for so long. I can feel it beckoning to me. This is it . . . I just know it!" There was only one minor hitch: I didn't have the experience.

For years, I had worked in the public relations field as a writer, and I was feeling burnt out. In 1991, I was ready for a change, but was beginning to learn that it's not so easy to switch careers, especially without retraining. I had been casting about for something to do that would tap into my skills and expertise when I saw the ad. This job sounded perfect. I was an inveterate lecture-attender and a voracious reader. Putting together lectures and seminars didn't sound difficult; it sounded like fun! But how was I going to circumvent the "experience required" part? First things first: I called the number in the ad and talked my way into an interview.

My interviewers were impressed with my credentials but concerned about my lack of programming experience. I assured them that I could handle the demands of the position, and they were swayed by my confidence. I got the job.

But my confidence foundered almost as soon as I arrived at the office on the first day. "Oh, so you're *Helene Isaac's* successor," one elderly employee said with concern. "What big shoes to fill. She was a phenomenon!" Another said tactlessly, "Well, I do feel sorry for you. There's nobody in this world like Helene Isaacs!" Then a third remarked, "Well, a hearty welcome to our organization, which, you'll find, is a great place to work." Then she shook her head mournfully. "But it sure hasn't been the same since Helene Isaacs left!"

I was ready to pick up my purse and flee. How was I ever going to compete with the phantom Helene?

Then I was ushered into my predecessor's office and didn't know whether to laugh or cry. A veritable paper mountain of letters, memos, brochures, and newspaper clippings—three feet high at least—covered Helene's desk. "Uh . . . why don't you spend the day cleaning off Helene's desk," suggested the personnel director, embarrassed, hastily backing out of the room. "She was very brilliant and creative but a trifle . . . disorganized," she said in explanation as she retreated.

I put down my handbag and stared in dismay at the daunting paper mountain. What a way to begin! How was I expected to know which papers should be saved and which could be discarded? Couldn't this venerable icon at least have had the decency to clean off her desk before she left? I sighed. Just then, another staff member stuck her head into my room and said, "Oh, you're Helene's replacement; I want to welcome you. Helene was here eighteen years, you know. Do you think you could stay that long?"

I didn't think I could stay for another hour. I picked up the phone and called my friend Rose. "This was a terrible mistake!" I wailed. "How could I have had the nerve to even think for a minute that I could undertake a job for which I have no real experience! I never coordinated an all-day conference before . . . I must have been out of my mind to think I could do it. I better get out of here fast before they discover what a hoax, what a charlatan, what a fraud I really am. In fact, I think I'm actually going to pick up my handbag and go home right now!"

"Whoa! Wait a minute!" cautioned my friend. "Where's the fearless 'can do' spirit that's always infused your life? Where's your desire to stretch, to expand? Where's the woman I know and love who welcomes a challenge and a chance to grow? You *can* do it! All beginnings are hard."

"Yeah, you're right," I conceded sheepishly. "I shouldn't give up so fast. But what about this pile of papers I have to contend with?" I moaned. "What am I going to do with those?"

"Hey," Rose said, "why don't you look at it as a learning experience? Work your way through the stack very slowly, read each paper carefully, and by the time you're finished, I bet you'll know much more about the job than you did when you started."

I was inspired and heartened by her attitude. "You're right!" I exclaimed. "I'm going to see this as a challenge and a learning experience. I *won't* throw in the towel!" Blinking back my tears, I concentrated on going through the pile of papers stacked high on the desk.

When I finally got to the very last one, I blinked again. But this time it was in wonder and awe.

I picked up the old, yellowing, tattered piece of paper, dated, incredibly, 1956, and, shaking my head in amazement, knocked on a colleague's door. "Can I help you?" she asked cheerfully.

"Can you tell me who this woman was?" I asked pointing to the paper. "In the first paragraph, she's identified as Judith Mandelbaum, but in the third paragraph she's referred to as Mrs. Mordechai Mandelbaum."

"Oh, Judith Mandelbaum—she was director of programming, too. She was Helene's predecessor, and she was excellent! She retired in 1962, when Helene took over. She was an icon of the organization and she was here for ages!"

I returned to my office, smiling and relieved. And I knew: everything would work out fine, everything would be all right. I would meet the challenge of my new position and I would succeed. I would be here for a while, I was sure.

You see, *my* own English first name is Judith; my *husband's* is Mordechai. And our family name is . . . Mandelbaum!

It's five years now, and I'm still at the job.

— *Yitta Halberstam Mandelbaum*

Comment:

Was this "coincidence" a reassuring tap on the shoulder? Here, engulfed by waves of self-doubt, the new employee questions the wisdom of moving into a new field. Every reference to the legendary Helene Isaacs is another assault on her self-confidence and weakens her resolve to stay on the job. But when she uncovers a link to a predecesor, she finds the reasurance she has been seeking. And, as a result of undertaking the job, which puts her into constant contact with celebrity authors, she becomes inspired and emboldened to write a book of her own — the very one you're reading now!

*T*om Stonehill* had been driving for several hours when he was overcome with the urge to go to the bathroom. It was late at night and all the gas stations he passed were closed. As time wore on, he became increasingly desperate. Finally, Tom exited the highway and drove into the first town along the road. There, he searched for a place that had facilities open to the public.

As he drove, his physical need took on heightened urgency and he started to pick up speed. Just as he began to accelerate, he heard someone on a loudspeaker instructing him to pull over to the side. It was the town sheriff. The sheriff got out of his car and approached Tom. "How fast do you think you can drive around here?" he asked in a formidable tone.

"Sir," apologized Tom, "I never drive this fast, but you see, right now I am in dire need of a bathroom."

The sheriff noted the sincerity in Tom's voice and took pity on him. "I believe there may be something open if you continue on down this road," he said, pointing straight ahead. "But you gotta watch the speed limit!" he added.

"I will," replied Tom, relieved and glad to be moving on.

Moments later, Tom spotted a light in the distance. He was sure he was approaching a twenty-four hour grocery store. But the closer he came to his destination, the more it became clear that he was headed toward a funeral parlor. Tom felt hesitant about using their facilities, but his urge was too strong to ignore. He drove up to the entrance, parked his car, and walked in.

Once inside, he was greeted warmly. "Welcome. Would you please sign in?" said Mr. Gifford*, the funeral director.

"Uh . . . I'm just here to use the bathroom," Tom said apologetically. "May I?"

"Of course you may," responded the director, "but please sign in first." Tom couldn't figure out why it was necessary to write his name down, but he did as he was told and hoped that would end the matter. Tom was about to ask the whereabouts of the men's room when Mr. Gifford said, "Please write in your full address as well."

"But why do you need my address?" asked Tom, perplexed, "I'm just here to use the bathroom for a minute."

"Please, sir, fill in the information," came the reply.

"What the heck?" Tom muttered to himself as he wrote. Then he followed as Mr. Gifford led him to the men's room.

Before leaving the funeral parlor, Tom stopped for just a moment to pay his respects to the deceased. On his way out of the building, Tom saw the sheriff. "Thank you," he nodded to Mr. Gifford and the sheriff, and with that, Tom was off and on his way back home.

Three weeks later, Tom received a phone call from a man unknown to him, who identified himself as an attorney. "I represent the funeral home where you stopped to use the washroom a few weeks ago," the man said. "You need to be in my office this Thursday at 2:00 P.M."

Tom was shaken. Alarmed, he asked, "Please tell me, did I do something wrong? Will I need a lawyer?"

"No, that won't be necessary," the attorney assured him. "Just be prompt," he said. The attorney gave Tom his address and then hung up the phone.

For the next few days, Tom was on edge. "What could I possibly have done? Why would they call me in?" he wondered aloud. That Thursday, he drove to the attorney's office with apprehension.

Tom found the office building as instructed. With bated breath and a pounding heart, he knocked on the front door. "Come in," said the secretary. The attorney stepped out, formal introductions were made, and then Tom was directed to the office. Once inside, Tom was surprised to see both the sheriff and Mr. Gifford present.

"Please be seated," began the attorney. "I have been authorized by the court to read the last will and testament of Mr. Stanley Murrow*." The attorney picked up the guest book that Tom had signed. He turned to the funeral director, pointed at Tom and asked, "Is this the man who signed the book?"

"Yes," said the funeral director. Then the attorney looked at Tom and began, "I guess you didn't know Mr. Murrow*. He was a very wealthy man. He owned most of this town. However, he did not have any family and was universally disliked, practically shunned by the townspeople. Mr. Murrow has authorized me to be his executor." The attorney picked up a document and continued. "This is the shortest will I have ever drawn up. It reads simply: 'Everyone hated my guts, and no one ever got any money from me when I was alive. So any person who comes to my funeral is obviously someone who had some compassion for an old coot like me. I hereby bequeath my entire estate with all my holdings to be divided equally among those who actually attended my funeral.'"

The attorney then looked straight at Tom. "Yours was the only signature that appeared in the register book," he said. "Therefore. . . ."

Comment

There are misers who hoard their wealth, ensuring that no one will have pleasure from it but themselves. Financially, they may be well off, but spiritually they are bankrupt. Conversely, there are those who are in need, yet give of themselves generously and are blessed with an abundance of spirit. Who then is really the rich one? And who is really poor?

It was Pam Altschul's first day as a freshman at the University of Michigan, far from her parents' home on Long Island. It was also Rosh Hashonah, the first day of the Jewish New Year. While her roommates were unpacking and just beginning to get acquainted, Pam was preparing to leave for the synagogue. She would have liked to stay and take part in the introductions but she felt compelled to attend services instead. It was a custom that she had observed since childhood.

Pam exited the dorm from the far right side of the building feeling somewhat lonely and isolated. As she looked around at her new surroundings, she noticed a young woman leaving from the far left side of the same building at the same time. Both were obviously dressed to attend a religious service. They crossed the lawn diagonally and met one another at midpoint. There was an awkward silence between the two women as they walked along side by side. Finally, Pam spoke first. "Hello," she began, "my name is Pam."

"Pam?" came the startled response. "Why, my name is Pam too!"

"Are you by any chance going to the synagogue?" asked the first Pam.

"Yes, I am," came the reply from the second.

A lively conversation ensued. The two Pams quickly discovered that they had much in common. They shared a common middle initial as well as first names. They had both grown up in the same unique type of ranch house in neighboring towns. Both of their mothers were teachers. Both of their respective best friends from high school were now best friends in college. And both had only sisters.

By the time they reached the synagogue doors, one more commonality was revealed. At the start of that day, both women had felt overwhelmed by the sea of new faces and both had wished that they would make at least one new friend. Indeed, that walk was the beginning of a friendship that deepened and became stronger as the years wore on.

Today, one Pam lives in Connecticut and the other in New York. Despite the distance, they continue to be the best of friends, and every Rosh Hashonah, they share the most heartfelt wishes for the New Year.

Comment

Just when you think you are alone, take one more step, walk one more block, hold on to hope just a bit longer, for just around the next corner, there may be a new friendship waiting to begin.

Although I lost both my parents two years ago—they died within a few months of each other—I remember the circumstances surrounding my mother's death more vividly, because they were unusual and striking.

I am a great fan of the Christian evangelical singer Curtis Stiegers. His music has always had the power to uplift and comfort me in the worst of times. When my mother was rushed to the hospital one evening, before entering the ambulance I paused to grab my black tote bag, which hangs in the corner in the front hall. It contains my Walkman and several of Stiegers's tapes. I had the feeling that I would be needing to listen to his music that night.

All night long, as doctors worked over my mother, who had had a stroke, I listened to my Curtis Stiegers tapes in the hospital waiting room. Kind nurses brought me coffee from time to time and offered me their company, but the solace I sought was from Stiegers's music. Early in the morning, the battery in the Walkman must have run out, because the music suddenly came to an abrupt halt. Startled out of my anesthetized state, I automatically glanced down at my watch and was surprised to note that it was 4:41. The night had passed more swiftly than I had ever imagined possible, and I got up to check on my mother's condition. As I walked towards the nurse's station, I saw a body draped with a sheet being wheeled out of a room. It was my mother.

When I received the death certificate, I saw to my shock that the time of death had been 4:41. Exactly the time that my Walkman battery had run out and Curtis had stopped singing!

— *Ellen Palmer**

ᕦᖳᖯ

Comment:
"There is a time to sing and a time to weep," Ecclesiastes said. There are moments in our lives when we *must* embrace the hard times and the pain. Since it was no longer appropriate for the joyous music to play, it stopped. The time to confront the tragedy and to mourn had arrived.

*M*y husband is the ultimate Good Samaritan. Wherever he goes, wherever he happens to be, he's always performing random acts of kindness, often for people he doesn't know, and sometimes for people he doesn't *even see*. Most of the time I am proud and gratified to be married to such a man, but once in a while I get annoyed when I think he's being excessive. When this spirit moves me—on rare occasions I must admit—I start to sulk, fume, and—if what he's done really strikes me as extravagant—boil over with rage. "Hmpph," I'll sputter indignantly, "this is all very nice, but when was the last time somebody did something like this for you or for me? Are you the only Good Samaritan left in town?"

But last week these doubts were given short shrift by a universe far wiser than I.

My husband and I were idly window-shopping one day in a local business district, where cars were parked along the curb next to meters. Suddenly, we noticed a grim-faced meter maid stomping determinedly down the street, studying each meter intently, pen poised, prepared to write tickets. My husband immediately pulled out all the change in his pockets and began running down the street, frantically inserting quarters into all the expired meters, pre-empting the meter maid.

When she finally advanced upon him it was with raised eyebrows and a scowling face; he in turn flashed her a triumphant grin and a roguish wink. From a distance, I watched my husband tenderly. It struck me that he was engaging in the highest form of charity: none of the people whose cars he had saved from being ticketed would ever know their benefactor; they probably wouldn't even know they had one! I was proud of him, to be sure. Still, when he returned from his labors, that little, cynical voice that I contend with all the time had the final word: "That was beautiful, honey . . . but when was the last time somebody did that for you or for me?"

The next day, I was shopping again, this time in a different business district, and parked my car next to a meter. In a dress shop filled with luscious creations I lost all sense of time and, when I glanced down at my watch, I realized with a start that my time on the meter must have expired. I hurried out of the store and ran towards my car, parked a block away. With a sinking heart, I saw a meter maid advancing towards the car.

Now, my husband, a perfectly reasonable man in all other respects, gets totally enraged when I get a parking ticket. He considers it the height of irresponsibility and a horrible waste of money besides. A parking ticket means at least three hours of serious fighting, followed by a full day of shameful recriminations and mournful head-shaking. I have learned (painfully) to avoid getting parking tickets, at all costs.

But when I saw the meter maid just a few feet away from my car, I knew all hope was lost. There was no way I could get to the meter before she did. I almost wept in consternation.

Suddenly, I saw an unfamiliar-looking man sprint across the street, dash over to my meter, and insert a quarter. At that point the meter maid approached, and he smiled broadly at her. Then he turned and strode quickly down the street. I rushed after him to thank him, wondering, "Who could it be? Is it someone who knows me . . . maybe a neighbor, a relative . . . someone who recognized the car and wanted to help me out?" But when I caught up with him and called to him to stop, it was a complete stranger who turned around.

"You just rescued me from the meter maid!" I bubbled. "Thank you so much—I can't believe you did that! Do you know my husband by any chance, and did you recognize our car? What made you do it?"

"Oh, I don't know your husband and I don't know your car," he said. "But I happened to see the meter maid coming, and I thought, what a shame—she's going to ticket that car. All it cost me was twenty-five cents to save you from a twenty-five-dollar ticket."

I was overwhelmed, and I couldn't thank the man enough. "Oh, it's OK really," he said. "I do this all the time!"

— *Yitta Halberstam Mandelbaum*

*S*everal years ago, the writer Deborah Wilde* found herself walking the streets of a small backwater village in England, a place that was obscure and unknown to tourists. Thousands of miles away from her home in New York, Deborah was visiting her in-laws, who lived in the hamlet. The visit had turned into a nightmare — her strife-filled marriage was unraveling, and that day she had quarreled with both her husband and his parents. To escape a volatile situation, she had announced her intention of taking a walk (even though it was raining hard) and had stepped out into the downpour.

"What am I doing in this godforsaken place, anyway?" she thought, dispirited. "Just what is the *point* of my being here?"

Meanwhile, a man by the name of Richard Wilson* was walking the streets of the same village, in an equally gloomy frame of mind. He too was from New York, and had come to meet his biological parents, who had given him up for adoption at birth. Many years before, he had embarked on an exhaustive search to find them, and he had finally traced them to this town. He had been in an excited, even exhilarated state when he rang the doorbell of their home, visions of a warm, loving reunion filling his imagination. The reception accorded him, however, had turned out to be quite different. His biological parents had been cold, even hostile, rebuffing all overtures. After fruitlessly trying to break down their reserve, he had finally left with an aching heart. His trip across the Atlantic had been for nought; the dreams that had stretched across years had turned to dust. "God, I feel so terribly alone," he said to himself in despair. "I feel like killing myself! They were so mean—my own parents, my own flesh and blood. What I wouldn't give right now for one friendly face, one warm smile! Isn't there anyone in the world who would be happy to see me?"

Just then, Deborah and Richard passed each other in the swirling mist. Their eyes locked. They froze. Then Deborah ran toward Richard, enfolding him in a fervent embrace. "Richard!" she shrieked happily. "Oh God, Deborah!" he wept in relief.

The two were cousins, and close friends. Deborah's question had been answered. So had Richard's. Simultaneously.

The true purpose of Deborah's presence in this town had finally been revealed. She was there to give Richard solace at a time when he needed it most.

Comment:

Both Richard and Deborah were undergoing variations of the exact same experience: the painful unraveling of lifelong dreams and hopes, the loss of a certain identity, the need for a final, excruciating confrontation with the past. When they "stumbled" upon each other, they were able to give each other the comfort both so desperately needed.

A well-known editor at a major publishing house was constantly besieged by writer friends who bombarded him with book proposals and unsolicited manuscripts. One acquaintance was especially persistent, and petitioned the editor tenaciously to consider his novel. Finally, he reluctantly agreed to take a look at it. "Everyone thinks he's a writer!" grumbled the editor as he grudgingly removed the manuscript from the slush pile.

Pleasantly surprised to discover that the book had merit, the editor decided to take it home for further study. The 400-page manuscript had been enclosed in a gift box, and the editor placed the box on the front seat of his car. Before heading home, however, he made a stop at a local restaurant for a quick bite. He parked on a dimly lit street and rushed into the eatery, forgetting to lock the car doors.

When he returned to the car half an hour later, he discovered that it had been broken into and his radio removed. Worse—far worse—the gift box containing the manuscript was gone. The radio could easily be replaced, but the writer had told him repeatedly that he had failed to make a duplicate of the manuscript, and that the copy the editor had in his possession was the *only* copy.

And now it had been stolen!

The editor's heart sank. How was he going to tell his friend that the book he had worked on for three years — his magnum opus, his masterpiece — was gone? No, it wasn't right to do it now, from a pay phone on the street, with traffic in the background. He would wait until he got home, and call him from the relative calm of his study. He knew he was procrastinating, but he couldn't help it; that call would be one of the hardest things he had ever had to do in his life.

The moment he arrived home, the phone rang. It was the writer, his voice indignant. "Oh," said the editor, taken aback, "I was just going to call you . . ."

"Yeah, and I know about what," interrupted the writer angrily, "and I think it's just disgusting!"

The editor was puzzled; how could the writer have known about the stolen manuscript? He hadn't told anyone yet. "What do you mean?" he asked.

"What do I mean? You know very well what I mean!" the writer exploded. "So you didn't like my book, fine . . . you have a right to your opinion. But did you have to show your contempt by throwing it into my backyard . . . into the mud?"

Having been chased by a pair of eagle-eyed cops, the thieves who had broken into the editor's car had tossed the weighty manuscript over a fence into the nearest backyard . . . The *writer's* backyard.

Subsequently, the novel was published.

*J*ulia Dixon* had just accidentally locked herself out of her house when the mailman came up the drive. "Mrs. Dixon!" he exclaimed in concern. "You look upset. What's the matter?"

"Oh, I don't know what I'm going to do," she wailed, wringing her hands nervously. "The door locked behind me, and my neighbor, who keeps a duplicate for me, is out of town. My husband has a key, but he's at an all-day conference at a hotel downtown, and I doubt I can reach him. How am I going to get back in?"

The mailman tried to calm the woman, and advised her to call a locksmith. "I guess that's my only recourse," she agreed, "but to tell you the truth, they charge an arm and a leg and I really can't afford an extra expense right now. Things have been tight."

The mailman commiserated with her, but pointed out that she had no choice. "Look, I better be on my way," he said, "but here's your mail. Who knows? Maybe there'll be some good news inside one of the letters to cheer you up!"

Julia looked through the envelopes. There was one from her brother Jonathan. He had visited the family the previous week and had stayed for a few days. "I wonder why he's writing so soon?" she murmured. As she tore open the letter, a key fell into her palm.

"Dear Julia," the letter read. "Last week, when I was staying at your house and you were out shopping, I accidentally locked myself out. I asked your neighbor for your duplicate, but forgot to return it. So I'm enclosing it now."

୧୧୫୬

Comment:

When you face a closed door and you're feeling hopeless, know that all doors can be opened, making way for you to step right in.

*A*s a major dress manufacturer in Canada, I sold some goods to a small retail operation in Montreal, which was owned by a man who was a member of my synagogue. I had heard that he was an upright, respectable man who ran an ethical business, so I gave him credit. According to the terms we had initially agreed to, he was supposed to pay his bill of $8,724 sixty days after receiving my shipment. I was very disheartened when my bookkeeper told me that he was delinquent on his payment.

We sent out three notices, which he ignored. Finally, I picked up the phone and called him. "What's going on?" I inquired. "Look," he sighed, "I'm really sorry but I can't pay my bill. Business is terrible, and I may have to close. I don't have a penny to my name."

I didn't know what to do, so I consulted my rabbi. "Should I take him to court?" I asked. "After all, $8,724 is not a negligible amount; I really need that money! On the other hand, I feel bad for him; he's down on his luck—what can he really do?" The rabbi didn't give me much concrete advice. "Follow your heart!" he counseled.

I wrestled with myself for a long time, and finally concluded that I didn't have the heart to sue the man. I heard later that he closed his business. He moved away to a different section of the town, joined another synagogue, and I lost track of him. Several years passed, and my business prospered.

One day, I received a call from a woman whose name I didn't recognize, who asked if she could come up to my office to see me. She was deliberately vague about her intentions, but my curiosity was piqued, so I agreed to see her. When she arrived, she revealed her identity: she was the daughter of the man who still owed me the $8,724.

"All these years, my father has felt terribly guilty about the debt he owes you," she said. "He went bankrupt and was never able to stage a comeback. He still doesn't have any money, but he asked me to give you this instead." She then pulled a piece of jewelry out of her pocketbook and handed it to me.

It was a gold bracelet studded with diamonds. "It's a family heirloom," she told me, "and practically the only thing of value my father has left. He asked me to give it to you with his sincerest apologies and greatest hope that it's worth something. He doesn't know how valuable it is, but he's hoping it will bring you at least part of what he owes you." At this point, I didn't want to take it, but she insisted.

I don't know much about jewelry, but I doubted that the piece was really valuable. I tossed it into a drawer and forgot about it. A few days later, I remembered it and showed it to my father, who was also quite skeptical about its possibilities. However, he suggested that it wouldn't hurt to go to an expert he knew for an appraisal.

The appraiser examined the bracelet carefully and at length. Finally, after much time had elapsed, he turned to us and said excitedly, "This is a really valuable piece! It's worth much more than you imagined. As a matter of fact, I would like to buy it from you. I'm prepared to give you $8,724."

The exact amount, to the dollar, that the man had owed me!

— *Patrick Simone* *

Comment:
In our dog-eat-dog world, someone who acts generously can be made to feel like a patsy. For doing the right thing, the manufacturer has clearly won accolades and applause from a higher power.

*A*lthough Cheryl McAdam* fervently loved her adopted family, she was tormented by questions about the biological one she had never known. She had been raised lovingly by doting adoptive parents who had spoiled her incessantly; she had received warmth and devotion in abundance; and she lacked for nothing. Still, despite all the blessings in her life, she could not help but obsess about her past.

Who were her natural parents? Why had they given her up? How could they have given up their own child? What were they like? And—most important—what would her life had been like had she grown up with them instead of with her adopted family? These questions plagued her continually as she fantasized about the life that might have been.

Finally, when she was twenty-one, married, and had given birth to a daughter, Kayla, she resolved to uncover the truth. She approached her adoptive parents and asked for their permission to launch a search. She loved them very much, she insisted, but her daughter's birth had reawakened her need to know her heritage. Compassionate, her adopted parents agreed to help her travel back to her roots.

Hers was a successful search — more successful than in her wildest dreams. More than anything else, it brought her a certain validation for which she had always hungered — a validation that finally laid to rest all her doubts, questions, conflicts, and fears.

This is what she discovered:

Her natural mother's first name — Anne — was almost the same as her adopted mother's, Anna. Her natural father, who had married her natural mother a year after they had given her up, was named John — the same as her adoptive father, Johnnie. Her two natural siblings bore the same first names as her adopted siblings — Carol and Wayne. And finally, when her natural sister, who had gotten married the previous year (about the same time she had) had given birth — to twins — she had named them *Kyle* and *Kaylee*, not one but two variations of her own daughter's name — Kayla.

Cheryl returned home happy, assured that her placement in her adopted family had not only been right . . . it had been destined!

Comment:

Cheryl is haunted by concerns of dislocation and displacement. Perhaps, she wonders, her destiny would have been quite different had she been raised by another family . . . her biological one. However, the coincidences convey "You were in the right family all along!" The parallels here are so strong and obvious, there's no possibility of misinterpreting them. As a result of these "coincidences," the young woman acquired newfound serenity and peace of mind, and her anxiety about having grown up in the wrong family was forever dispelled.

In the 1930s, Rabbi Samuel Shapira, the distinguished chief rabbi of the Polish village of Prochnik, was in the habit of taking long, invigorating walks into the countryside. The rabbi, who was known for his warm, loving, and compassionate ways, always made a point of greeting everyone whose path he crossed—Jew and non-Jew alike—and, adhering to a Talmudic dictum, always tried to greet them first.

One of the people he regularly greeted on his daily walks was a peasant by the name of Herr Mueller, whose farm lay on the outskirts of the town. Every morning, Rabbi Shapira would pass the farmer as he diligently worked in his fields. The rabbi would nod his head and expansively boom in a hearty voice, "Good morning, Herr Mueller!"

When the rabbi had first embarked on his morning constitutional and had begun greeting Herr Mueller, the farmer had turned away in stony silence. Relations between Jews and gentiles in this village were not particularly good, and friendships were rare. But Rabbi Shapira was not deterred or discouraged. Day after day, he would greet the silent Herr Mueller with a hearty hello, until, finally convinced of the rabbi's sincerity, the farmer began returning the greeting with a tip of his hat and a hint of a smile.

This routine went on for many years. Every morning, Rabbi Shapira would call out, "Good morning, Herr Mueller!" And every morning Herr Mueller would tip his hat and yell back, "Good morning, Herr Rabiner!" This scenario stopped when the Nazis came.

Rabbi Shapira and his family, together with all the other Jewish residents of the village, were shipped to a concentration camp. Rabbi Shapira was transferred from one concentration camp to the next until he reached his final destination point: Auschwitz.

As he disembarked from the train, he was ordered to join the line where selection was taking place. Standing in the back of the line, he saw from a distance the camp commandant's baton swing left, swing right. He knew that left signified certain death, but right bought time and possible survival.

His heart palpitating, he drew closer to the commandant as the line surged forward. Soon it would be his turn. What would be the decree? Left or right?

He was one person away from the man in charge of the selection, the man whose arbitrary decision could send him into the flames. What kind of man was this commandant, a man who could so easily send thousands of people a day to their deaths?

Despite his own fear, he looked curiously, almost boldly into the face of the commandant as his turn was called. At that moment, the man turned to glance at him, and their eyes locked.

Rabbi Shapira approached the commandant and said quietly, "Good morning, Herr Mueller!" Herr Mueller's eyes, cold and unfathomable, twitched for a fraction of a second. "Good morning, Herr Rabiner!" he answered, also very quietly.

And then he swung his baton forward. "Recht!" he shouted with a barely perceptible nod. "Right!" To . . . life!

Comment:

Who would have thought a simple "Hello" could save a life? Yet sometimes the smallest of actions (or at least actions that we perceive to be small) can result in the greatest—and gravest—of consequences. The rabbi sowed the seeds of his redemption for years by engaging in polite pleasantries with a person whom others might have deemed an inconsequential peasant. Could he ever have envisioned that one day this man would quite literally hold his fate in his hands?

*T*om MacEnvoy* hated this daughter Trisha's cat. She had picked up the stray in the school's courtyard, promptly fallen in love with it, and brought it home, pleading, "I know you swore no more pets after the hamster disaster, Dad, but please let me keep him! I love him so much!"

"But Trisha," her father objected, "he's just a plain old alley cat. If you want a cat, let me at least get you a Persian."

"No, this is the one I want! When I saw him in the yard, he came right up to me, rubbing against me, meowing and purring. We're right for each other, Dad . . . we connect!" Tom MacEnvoy succumbed to his daughter's soft entreaties, but whenever he saw the cat, he scowled and turned away in distaste.

One morning, Tom found debris from the litter box scattered all over the floor of the dining room. Seizing on this as an excuse, he said to his daughter, "That does it! The cat goes tomorrow!"

"Please, Dad, this is the first time he's done anything like this. Something seems to be the matter with him today, he's acting so peculiar. Please give him a chance."

"No chance," Tom bellowed. "Try finding him a home today. Tomorrow he's out!"

Late that night, Trisha was startled out of her sleep by a loud thump and a flying body that hurtled into her bed. "Hey, what's going on?" she muttered as she looked in disbelief at her cat's arched body and raised fur. The cat always slept curled up on an afghan in the corner of her room. What was it doing in her bed? And it was acting so strangely, too, making angry, hissing sounds, circling wildly on her quilt. "Hey, get out of here!" she said sleepily, gently shoving the cat off her bed, pulling the covers up over her head. In a second, he was back, hissing louder than before. "What's the matter with you?" she shouted, pushing him off again, trying to get back to sleep. When he returned a third time, she threw up her hands, yelled, "OK, I give up" and climbed into her sister's bed on the other side of the room.

Just then, the floor began to vibrate and shake in an all-too-familiar manner. Books slipped from shelves, lamps crashed to the floor, objects tumbled, and furniture slid over the room. A huge chest of drawers, jarred from its usual position against the wall, toppled across the bed where only seconds before Trisha had been sleeping.

It was the Northridge, California earthquake of 1994, and the "plain old alley cat" had saved Trisha's life. Needless to say, the cat has since become a permanent member of the MacEnvoy household.

Comment:

Life is very mysterious and awesome, and you never know from where your salvation will come. Sometimes, it comes from the most unlikely of sources. Let us learn to regard all living things as divine and gifts from God . . . and treat them accordingly!

he tale has the elements of a classic mystery: a grieving widow; a misidentified body; a key, which, despite lottery-like odds, fits the wrong door; and a happy ending, as the husband and wife, having each learned the other is not dead, vow never to take each other for granted.

No, it is not a movie (not yet, anyway); it really happened to a Houston couple, Jose and Herlinda Estrada.

At about 5 P.M. on Feb. 11, Jose Estrada, 48, left his house, headed for a nearby jogging track. Telling his family he would be back shortly, he climbed into his 1988 burgundy Chevrolet truck and left.

About 50 minutes later, Herlinda Estrada's concentration on the National Basketball Association's All-Star Game was shattered by every wife's nightmare: a stony-faced constable was at the front door.

"I have a 27-year-old son," Mrs. Estrada said, "so the first thing I thought was, 'He had a wreck.' But then the constable said, 'What is your husband's name?' And then, 'Does he have a red truck?'"

"When I said 'yes,' he said, 'I'm sorry ma'am, he's had a heart attack.'"

Told that Jose's condition was grave, Mrs. Estrada, who like her husband is Catholic, called a priest to administer last rites. Then, Mrs. Estrada "drove like crazy" to nearby Memorial Hospital Southeast, where she was ushered into a small consultation room, and told that she was too late; Jose Estrada had died.

The constable—the same officer who had come to Mrs. Estrada's house—escorted the grieving wife to a small room, where she identified the body. Then she signed the death certificate and returned to the waiting room, where she asked the constable to make the first few calls to family and friends. He did so.

Within minutes, family and friends began gathering to comfort the Estradas. Thirty minutes later, in walked a relative no one expected: Jose Estrada himself.

"At first it didn't register," Mrs. Estrada recalled. "and then I started screaming, 'You're alive, you're alive! They told me you were dead.' And he said, 'I'm O.K.—I was worried about you.'"

Jose Estrada had just rushed to the hospital after someone told him that his wife had a heart attack.

How did this all come about? Elementary, Watson; while Jose Estrada was jogging, another runner had a coronary. Emergency medics and the constable were summoned, but could find no identification on the man. The only clue was a set of General Motors keys, which the constable tried in the doors of G.M. vehicles in the area.

Despite 26,000-to-1 odds, the keys opened the wrong G.M. vehicle—Mr. Estrada's. A license check led the constable to the Estradas' house.

And the misidentified body?

"You just have to put yourself in that state of mind," Mrs. Estrada said. "There was tape on his eyes and mouth, so I couldn't tell if he had a mustache. He had the same shoes, same radio, same shorts as my husband. He even had the same kind of belt. So I said, 'Let me see the hands and feet.' " He had the same feet.

"What's so funny is I asked Constable Hernandez, 'Does he look Mexican?' And the constable said, 'Yes.' "

Jose Estrada, meanwhile, had returned from his jog to find the house curiously deserted. Then, the phone rang; it was his wife's boss, who had received a call from the hospital. "She said, 'Jose, you're alive!' " Mrs. Estrada related. "And then, she said 'Oh, my God—don't tell me it was Herlinda.' "

Mr. Estrada raced to the hospital, walked up to none other than the constable and told him he was looking for Herlinda Estrada. The constable pointed toward a consultation room filled with wailing friends and family. Expecting the worst, Mr. Estrada walked in.

After the Estradas' reunion, the constable returned to the track, where he found Mary Sammons looking for her husband, John. The constable broke the bad news once more and escorted Mrs. Sammons to the hospital, where she identified her husband's body.

"Let me tell you, we've changed some things since it happened," Mrs. Estrada said. For one, she said, they do not take each other for granted. And there were practical changes.

"We always look at what the other is wearing. He's put a silly yellow thing on the end of his keychain, so I can tell his keys. And he always takes an I.D. when he jogs."

❦

Comment:

Many of us "sleep-walk" through life. Sometimes we need a "jolt" to wake us from our apathy, our slumber, our automaton-like existence. This includes taking the people we love and need in our lives for granted. When such a jolt does occur, as in the jolt of coincidence that the Estradas experienced, we begin to look at our lives — and each other — with fresh eyes.

*M*ax left from New York City and had been traveling for several hours in the rain. His windshield wipers worked tirelessly as he headed toward a business meeting in Philadelphia. Sometime around midnight, Max got hungry and stopped at a roadside diner.

Max seated himself at the counter, alongside an elderly man with drooping shoulders, wearing tattered clothing. Max was moved by the presence of this individual, who looked as though he had walked too many miles in his lifetime. "Pretty nasty weather out there, isn't it?" said Max, attempting to make some conversation. The response was a grumble under the breath. The old man seemed to be too despondent to engage in dialogue. Max finished his meal and just before he left, he turned to the waitress and asked, "How much for a baked apple?"

"Two-fifty," she responded.

"Here," said Max, pulling out three singles. "This should cover the price of the apple and your tip." Then, pointing to the elderly man, Max said, "Now, please give it to that man and just say, 'It's on the house.'"

The waitress gave Max a warm smile and said, "Sure, will do." And with that, Max turned and left the diner.

As he traveled, Max thought about the gesture he had just made. "Why a baked apple?" he questioned himself. "Why didn't I buy him a cup of coffee?" Max pondered this seemingly illogical overture and delved into the workings of his mind until he came to a conclusion. "A cup of coffee from a stranger to a stranger may be a sweet gesture," he reasoned, "briefly noticed, but quickly forgotten. Whereas a fresh-baked apple might jostle the old man out of his stupor, even if only momentarily, and maybe even allow his spirits to be lifted." Max was satisfied with his reasoning as he continued on the long and narrow highway.

The night wore on. The endless white line became a challenge as Max struggled to stay alert and awake. He spoke out loud to the darkness but it was to no avail. His body was giving way, and despite all his efforts, the lull of sleep called to him. He was on Interstate 295 going south, when a huge Mac truck hit him on the side, pushing him off the edge of the road. Perhaps in the light of day, with different weather conditions, Max might have been able to handle the car and maintain his position on the highway. But now, Max's car skidded and slid into a ditch. At first Max was shocked. Within a few moments, he was unconscious.

In the dark of night, with torrents of rain pouring down, cars just zoomed by. No one seemed to notice the accident on the side of the road. Finally, after some time, a young man driving by spotted Max's car. He stopped and made his way towards the wreckage. The young man sized up the situation. He figured that with the weather being so bad, even if he managed to call 911, it would take a great deal of time for someone to arrive. Since he lived so close by, he decided to take Max, still unconscious, to his own home. There he would call for help.

Shortly after arriving in the stranger's home, Max regained consciousness. He opened his eyes to an unfamiliar face.

"My God," the stranger said, "that was some fall you and your car took! It was sure hard getting you out of that wreck and into this house, but I tell you, buddy, you were mighty close to death there! Now sit up and eat something my wife made for you." Max looked at the plate set down in front of him. Sitting on a glass dish was a fresh-baked apple.

Comment:

Passing on a kind gesture, enabling another's spirits to be lifted—these are goodly deeds. The word God is contained in the word good. When good is done, God is present and when God is present, miracles occur.

*T*he eminent psychiatrist Carl Jung had a lifelong interest in coincidences—an interest that was stimulated in part by his experiences during his therapeutic work with patients. In one such example, he was treating a fifty-year-old man whose wife had told him that following the deaths of both her mother and grandmother, a flock of birds had suddenly appeared outside the windows of the death chamber.

Jung's treatment of the man's neurosis was successful, and he was about to terminate the therapy when the patient suddenly began complaining about physical symptoms. Although the patient didn't appear to be in any imminent danger, some intuition led Jung to believe that the man was suffering from heart disease, and he immediately sent him to a specialist for a thorough checkup. After an extensive examination, the physician declared the man to be in good health, and wrote a note to Jung advising him of his diagnosis. On his way home from seeing the specialist, the man collapsed in the street.

As he was brought home dying, his wife was already in a high state of anxiety, because shortly after her husband had gone to the doctor, a huge flock of birds had alighted on their house. Remembering that, in the past, their sudden arrival had heralded the deaths of both her mother and grandmother, she naturally feared the worst—a fear that was justified and confirmed.

In a second instance of coincidence involving a patient, Jung was treating an extremely "resistant" woman, with whom he was unable to achieve any meaningful breakthrough. The difficulty lay in the fact that the patient—the beneficiary of an excellent education and a woman totally dominated by an implacably rationalistic spirit—thought she knew more than everyone else. Jung hoped fervently for an irrational and unexpected episode to occur that would pierce her intellectual armor. One day, the woman was in middle of reciting an odd dream to him—a dream in which she was given a costly piece of jewelry, a golden scarab (beetle)—when he heard a gentle tapping at the window. Turning around, Jung saw a strange-looking insect knocking against the windowpane from the outside. He opened the window and caught the creature as it flew in. It was a scarabeid beetle—an insect whose gold-green color makes it closely resemble that of a golden scarab. Jung handed the beetle to the patient with these words: "Here is your scarab." Years later, when he presented the case to other therapists, he noted that this startling coincidence had achieved what he himself had been unable to accomplish: it had broken down the patient's intellectual resistance and resulted in successful therapy. "But nothing quite like this has ever happened to me before or since," he declared.

So many other startling stories of coincidence were brought to Jung's attention during his lifetime that he dedicated enormous time and energy to studying this phenomenon, and coined a term to describe it. It was "synchronicity," a word common in our parlance today, which is defined as "meaningful coincidence of two or more events where something other than the probability of chance is involved."

ill and Jules ran an adult education school called the Learning Annex. While business was good, these two entrepreneurs wanted to expand, which meant getting lots more people to sign up for courses. But how could they make sure that everyone in New York City heard about their school? Breaking through all boundaries of thought and logic, they came up with a scheme that the city had never seen before. They planned on taking ten thousand one-dollar bills and affixing a sticker to each bill with information about the Learning Annex. The media alerted the public that on March 13, 1982, ten thousand one-dollar bills would be thrown off the Empire State building, and whoever was standing at Fifth Avenue and Thirty-fourth Street at that time would be able to keep as much money as they could catch. This would make for sensational publicity.

The New York media loved the idea, and reported it with lots of fanfare. Unfortunately, the police were not as enthusiastic. They were given strict orders to stop the event from happening, believing that thousands of people expecting to catch dollar bills would wreak havoc with traffic and create nightmarish circumstances.

Despite the official disapproval, Jules and Bill left their uptown office on the appointed date with two bags, loaded with ten thousand one-dollar bills. As they cruised down Fifth Avenue, making their way towards Thirty-fourth Street, they were followed by a bevy of reporters eager to capture each moment as it unfolded.

As they approached Thirty-fourth Street, they heard sirens. The reporters following the lead car had police band radios and were monitoring police activity in the area. The reporters started shouting, "Hey! Those sirens are for you guys!" Bill and Jules gulped and stared at the enormous crowd that had turned out for the event.

Then the unexpected occurred. Just as Bill and Jules were getting out of their car, two other men walked into a bank inside the Empire State Building, fired a shot in the air, and screamed, "This is a stickup!" They grabbed all the money they were handed, stuffed it into two bags, and ran out of the building and right into the street — which was teeming with police officers, reporters, and cameramen. Instead of the quiet getaway they had planned, this became one of the most publicized bank heists of all time.

What we now have are two groups of men, both carrying bags of money, one group running to take money away, and the other running to give it away. Both were on the same street corner at the very same moment.

Nobody could figure out what was going on. The cameramen didn't want to film the wrong people, the police didn't want to make a false arrest. The rest of the crowd was eagerly looking to see which pair was about to throw them money.

Finally, the bank robbers were apprehended. Meanwhile, Bill and Jules attempted to make their way into the building, but crowds of people closed in on them, trying to grab their bags. The same policemen who caught the criminals now had to extricate these two men from a crowd that wanted its fair share of the money. Amid the pandemonium, and much to the chagrin of thousands of onlookers, Bill and Jules were quickly hustled away by the police.

One lady who was trying to figure out what all the mayhem was about walked over to a police officer and asked, "What exactly is going on?" to which the officer answered, "Lady, if I told ya, ya wouldn't believe me."

꧁꧂

Comment:

God gives and God takes. The money comes and the money goes. It's all a circle. At times you want to take it and it's given to you, at other times you want to give it and you can't because it's been taken. We think we are our money and that our bank accounts state our worth. Money though, is like honey. It can drip into your life, and is sweet to behold. But its pleasure can be fleeting, leaving a taste for more. Money, now it's here, now it's gone. When you have some, pass some on.

In the winter of 1979, I began work with a Bowen coach (a family therapist) to change my position in a key triangle in my family. As a seasoned therapist myself, I understood that such a task was not to be taken lightly. Indeed, I fully anticipated encountering my own resistance to change, as well as my family's "change back!" maneuvers. Despite my intellectual sophistication, I was naive and ill-prepared for my venture. No one had warned me about cosmic countermoves.

What is a cosmic countermove? It is, in my opinion, nothing short of a "change back!" reaction from the cosmos itself. It is something different from, and greater than, the usual forms of resistance described in the literature on the family. A cosmic countermove issues from the gods themselves when we dare to disturb our universe or invite our clients to do the same. The case in point: my own family.

When I began working with my coach, my long-term goal was to establish an emotionally close relationship with both my mother and my father. Before this time, my relationship with my mother had been at my father's expense in that he had occupied an extreme, outside position in the family. In fact, fathers had occupied an outside position in my family for several generations, while mothers and daughters were bound together by unswerving loyalty. I simply did not contemplate having anything other than a distant relationship with my father.

Never did I so fully appreciate the power of resistance as when I proceeded to behave differently in this entrenched triangle. I vividly recall my starting point—a memorable visit from my parents in 1979, shortly after the birth of my second son. My mother was washing dishes in the kitchen, busily elaborating on my father's most recent manifestations of immaturity and insensitivity. My father was entertaining my husband, Steve, in the living room, undoubtedly making conspicuous displays of these same qualities. In the past, I would have joined forces with my mom. This time was different.

I still recall the terror in my bones as I told my mother that I didn't want to talk about Dad anymore. I went on to explain, with genuine warmth, that the older I became, the more I realized that I needed to have a relationship with *both* my parents—and that both of them were very important to me. When I was finished, my mother's anxiety was sky-high.

"You cannot know me," she said with uncharacteristic coldness, "if you are unwilling to hear the truth about your father!"

I put my arm around her and said, "Mom, I want to get to know *you* from my relationship with *you*—and I want to get to know *Dad* from my relationship with *Dad*." And so it went.

I had rehearsed the conversation in my head many times. Nonetheless, it felt like nothing short of treason.

"I'm going to give her cancer," I announced to my husband that evening.

My mother was not struck dead by my words, although she did have a predictably dramatic reaction, as she proceeded to test out whether I could be induced to reinstate the old pattern. The next morning, however, she appeared at the breakfast table looking cheerful and relaxed, having obviously enjoyed a good night's sleep. I, however, had not slept well at all, and when morning came, I discovered large red splotches on my arms. This new and colorful symptom was my first lesson in humility. My parents' resistance to change proved to be considerable—but less considerable, I confess, than my own.

So what's new? Any student of Family Systems Theory 101 knows that we can all be counted on to resist the very changes that we seek. I ask the reader to bear with me. This small slice of life is merely the historical backdrop against which I will illustrate a potent source of systemic resistance heretofore ignored in the family literature—the *cosmic countermove*.

Recently, I visited my parents in Phoenix, following news that my father—who prides himself on reaching the age of seventy-five without even a sniffle—had suffered a mild heart attack. This unexpected and unwelcome reminder of my father's mortality heightened my awareness that my parents were old and would not be around forever. During the visit, I felt especially loving towards them *both* and I was inspired to engage in a bold and courageous act.

Actually, bold and courageous acts were the name of the game since that first conversation with my mother in 1979. Of course, change occurs slowly, and rightfully so. But, as we will see, too bold a change may incur a *countermove* from the cosmos itself!

What, then, was my bold and courageous act? It was this: I asked my father if he would make me a gift of an old, prized Chinese bond. I told him that I would frame it and give it a place of honor in my home. This request may not sound particularly daring, or even noteworthy, to the reader. Nonetheless, the request and granting of this particular gift was a bold challenge to my family's long legacy of emotional distance between fathers and daughters.

My father carefully rolled the bond into a cardboard tube, so that I could hand-carry it safely on the airplane back to Topeka. His anxiety about this exchange was revealed only by the number of times he reminded me to keep it clean and frame it quickly, so that no harm would befall it.

As I boarded the airplane his final words were spoken with affection. "Now don't get chicken *schmaltz* (fat) on that bond, Harriet!" I had to smile at this reminder of my growing-up years in Brooklyn, and my father's chronic irritation at my habit of snacking while doing my homework, which sometimes led to chicken *schmaltz* finding its way onto my schoolwork.

I arrived home both pleased and anxious about this forbidden act of father–daughter intimacy. Where could I keep the bond until my schedule would permit a visit to the frame shop? I carefully removed it from the narrow cardboard tube and laid it flat on the carpeted floor of a remote attic room on the third floor of my large, old home. Our entire third floor is reserved for guests and this room is forbidden territory for the rest of the family. It is my private space and it has long been my custom to sort out my manuscripts and documents on the floor there.

Three weeks later, after receiving an inquiry from my father about the bond, I proceeded to retrieve it to bring to the framers. As I lifted the bond from its place, I could not register nor make sense of what my eyes saw. *The face of the bond was crinkled and stained.* But this was not possible! I examined the papers on the floor surrounding it and they were in perfect condition. I looked up at the ceiling directly above, half expecting to see a leak, but no leak was to be found. I stood staring at the bond in stunned disbelief and recalled my father's final words to me at the airport. Had the heavens dripped chicken *schmaltz* on his bond?

I rushed downstairs, bond in hand, where a friend was drinking tea in the dining room. She is almost thirty years my senior and wise in the ways of the world.

"What is this?" I demanded of her, as I thrust the stained bond under her nose.

My friend looked and sniffed—and then made her diagnostic pronouncement. "It's cat urine," she said blandly.

And so it was. My sons had left the front door open and one of the neighborhood cats that graced our front porch had made its way up two flights of stairs to find my father's bond and pee on it. How can we understand such an action! Did the cat not have 4,500 square feet of floor on which to pee, to say nothing of the countless papers that were spread about the floor of our attic rooms? How can we fathom such a choice? And how could I explain it to my father?

It was in contemplation of this event that I concluded that the concept of *cosmic countermove* should be added to the family systems literature. And yes, I believe there is a moral to my story: Dare *you* disturb the universe? Remember that multigenerational work is only for the boldest among us. Do not begin the journey, unless you are prepared to answer to the gods themselves!

As for my father, he took the news with surprising good humor. Perhaps—although I may be wrong—I detected a tad of relief in his voice.

Be it chicken *schmaltz* or cat pee . . . it is reassuring to know that some things never change!

— *Dr. Harriet Lerner*

Dr. Harriet Lerner is one of the foremost international authorities on women's psychology. She is the author of *The Dance of Deception*, *The Dance of Intimacy*, and *The Dance of Anger*. She is also a staff psychologist at the Menninger Clinic in Topeka, Kansas.

*T*ony Angelo* and his best friend George Petro* grew up in the Bensonhurst section of Brooklyn. The two dreamed about their future. "When I'm older, I'm going to join the navy," declared Tony, leaning against the banister in front of his house.

"And I'm going to join the army," said George.

It all seemed like wishful thinking at the time. But the years flew by and their boyhood dreams did become a reality.

Just before Tony entered the navy, George gave him a lavish farewell party and invited all their friends from the neighborhood. Everyone drank and danced for hours. As the party neared its end, George put his arm around Tony and said, "Buddy, I'm gonna miss ya." "Me too," said Tony. George was scheduled to leave for his army post within a few weeks. They recounted some of their better childhood memories, wished each other well, and said their goodbyes.

A few years passed. Tony's ship was docked in San Francisco. Like many of the other sailors, Tony wanted to take in the sights, but first he needed to tend to his wash. He found a nearby laundromat, but was disappointed to see that all its machines were in use. Wanting to explore the area in the small amount of time he had available, Tony wandered further into town. He found a laundromat in a cul-de-sac off a main thoroughfare.

Tony unloaded his clothing into the washing machine and then noticed that he didn't have the correct change. "Hey, buddy," he said, turning to the first person on his right, "got change of a dollar?" The stranger found the change, looked at Tony and said, "Here, that should do it." Tony thanked the stranger, and the two made eye contact. "GEORGE! IS THAT YOU?" shouted Tony. "TONY! IS THAT YOU?" came a resounding reply. They laughed and embraced each other warmly, in this place they had both found, far away from home.

❧

Comment:

The bonds we make in our youth are everlasting. They are patterned into the fabric of our lives. Time shifts, looks change, and much is left behind as we move along. But there are bits and pieces of our past that follow us through in life. Just like the woven threads of a tapestry that are integral to its design, friends from our childhood will continue to appear and reappear in our hearts and in our lives, because the bonds of youth remain.

*W*hile attending Princeton University, Cathy shared a dorm room with three roommates. Each one had her fair share of male admirers. In order to maintain some semblance of privacy, the girls would occasionally make arrangements to meet their respective dates at some anonymous location.

One summer's evening, Cathy set out on a blind date. She didn't have much faith that it would turn out well, but having agreed to the date, she wanted to keep her word. Cathy walked to the corner of Nassau Street and Washington Road. Her date was expected to be there at 8:00 P.M. Cathy had been told to look for a blue car whose driver would be wearing a fraternity sweater.

Everything seemed to go as planned. At a couple of minutes past eight, a blue car driven by a young man in a fraternity sweater pulled up alongside the curb. "Sorry I'm a little late—I got caught in traffic," he said apologetically.

"That's all right," Cathy said, pleasantly surprised that her date was good-looking.

Sometime after the movie and before dinner, the young man turned to his date and said, "By the way, how do you know Bob?"

"Bob? Who's Bob?" said Cathy.

"What do you mean, who's Bob? Bob is the one who set us up!" the young man said, raising a bushy eyebrow that accentuated his questioning glance.

"What are you talking about?" Cathy sputtered. "Jim set us up."

"Jim!" the young man answered. "Who's Jim?" A few more whos and whats and what-are-you-talking-abouts, and the puzzle was solved. They realized that another couple must have made arrangements to meet at the same time and at the same place. Which meant that they were each out with the "wrong" date.

Without skipping a beat, the young man turned to Cathy and said, "Look, I'm having a good time—want to continue?"

"Sure," she said, glad that he asked.

It's now ten years later, and they are happily married with three beautiful children.

❧

Comment:
At times, all we have to do in life is show up, be present, and allow the magic to unfold.

*I*n 1969, amidst the turbulence of the Vietnam War, a young Thai woman and a 20-year-old air force sergeant fell in love, lived together and gave birth to a baby boy. They named their son, Nueng.

At the end of the war, John Garcia, the father, and Pratorn Varanoot, the mother, faced each other, uncertain about the future. Transferring back to the States together seemed remote since the air force discouraged John from marrying a native, and Pratorn's family discouraged her from moving away. John moved back to America, leaving behind his ex-lover and his baby boy. He tried to maintain contact with them, but as time wore on, it became increasingly difficult to do so. Pratorn had married another U.S. soldier who repeatedly returned John's letters, unanswered. John wrote the Thai government in an attempt to locate them and retain some contact with his son. He never received a reply. The ties that bound this father and son were ultimately severed.

In 1996, a man drives down a highway in Pueblo, Colorado in his restored 1970 Nova. He happens to peer at the gas gauge that indicates the tank is half full. For some unexplainable reason, he decides to stop at a Total service station, a place he does not usually patronize. When it comes time to pay, once again he does something that he ordinarly wouldn't do: Despite having 30 dollars cash in his wallet, he pays by check. The young man behind the service counter looks down and notes the name on the check. With raised eyebrows he looks up at the man standing in front of him and asks, "Are you John Garcia?"

"Yes," comes the reply.

"Have you ever been in the air force?" inquires the young man.

"Yes," replies John, not thinking too much of the question.

"Have you ever lived in Thailand?" he continues.

"Yes," John says, as he steps back, wondering what this is all about.

"Do you have a son there?"

With great puzzlement, once again a resounding "Yes."

Now with halting breath and a racing heart, the cashier poses one more question, "What was his name?"

"Nueng," comes the reply.

Amidst the sea of anonymous commuters on highway 50, the young man then looks into the eyes of the stranger standing before him and simply states, "I am your son."

Comment:

People can leave each other, cross continents, sever ties. But if there are lessons to be learned from one another, if they are meant to be together, then time and distance dissolve and they are reunited once again.

$\mathcal{I}$*n* 1991, Debra Robinson* was dating Ed Wilson. They had been seeing each other for over three years. Although he had "popped the question" several times, she had avoided giving him an answer. Fearful, conflicted, and anxious about "tying the knot," she kept stalling. As a result, she was tormented and miserable.

One night, Chuck Anton, an old friend of her deceased father, Wayne Robinson, had a dream. In the dream, Wayne Robinson said, "Chuck, do me a favor. My daughter Debra is going out with someone, and this person is her destined one. Please find her and tell her that she should marry him, and that she's going to have a wonderful life! This match has my blessing and, for once, she should listen to her father!"

Chuck Anton woke up with a muffled scream. He hadn't seen Debra Robinson since her father had died ten years before. Shaken, he roused his wife and recounted the dream. She told him it was ridiculous and advised him to go back to sleep. He followed her counsel and soon forgot the entire episode.

A week later, Wayne Robinson reappeared in a new dream. "Chuck!" he expostulated, wagging an accusing finger. "You didn't do what I requested! How many times do I have to ask you to tell my daughter to marry the young man she's seeing!" Once again, Chuck awoke with a start, but this time he resolved to consult his priest.

"Look," said the priest after Chuck poured out his heart. "Find the girl, and ask her if she's currently seeing anyone seriously. If she isn't, say nothing. If she is, you have a responsibility to deliver her father's message."

The following Sunday, Debra Robinson lay on her bed, weeping. The night before, her younger sister Susie had gotten engaged. Although she was happy for her sister, the engagement had undeniably served to accentuate her own sense of aloneness and her anxiety about her relationship with Ed. Debra was in agony, and cried out, "Please God, help me figure out what to do! I beg you . . . send me a sign!" At that precise moment, the telephone rang.

"Debra?" an old, familiar voice inquired. "This is Chuck Anton . . ."

Three months later, Debra and Ed were married, and they have been living a fairy-tale life ever since!

Comment:

Many of life's decisions are painfully difficult to make, for none of us know what lies ahead. The jolt of coincidence can nudge us in the right direction. In this story, what was so comforting to Debra was not merely the wonderful message from her father, but that it arrived just when she needed it—and was most receptive to it. What impeccable timing! At the precise moment when Debra was feeling particularly lost, she received a loving, nurturing, supportive communiqué from her father that told her, "I'm with you! You are not alone!"

Barry and I were going steady in the fall of 1979. We were on our way to a restaurant one day when Barry decided to change course. He asked me if I would accompany him while he went to look at an old tenement house that was for sale. "I may be able to buy the building at a very good price," he said, "but first I need to check it out. Is it okay if we stop by for a quick look?" Though I was hungry, I agreed to go along. Experience had taught me that following Barry's lead usually led me down an interesting path.

After a short drive to the seedy part of town, we found ourselves in front of a dilapidated building. The windows were sealed off with odd pieces of iron and wood. The brick walls were covered with layers of spray paint.

"Are you sure we're in the right place?" I asked.

Barry checked the address again. "Yes, this is the building," he affirmed. Then, looking at me with an adventurous twinkle in his eye, he said, "Let's go inside."

"Are you serious?" I exclaimed, afraid to follow his dare. But my interest quickly got the better of my doubts and we ventured into the building.

As soon as we pried the front door open, we were immediately struck by an awful stench that permeated the hallway. "My God," I said, "are you sure we should go inside?"

"Let's go for it," Barry said. The hallway led to a narrow staircase. Together we climbed a flight of rickety steps. When we arrived at the first landing, we stood and gaped at the rat-infested debris. "How long do you think it's been since people have lived here?" I asked Barry.

Barry shook his head. "No idea," he said.

Thinking that the rest of the building must be very much like the first floor, we decided to leave and began to descend the decrepit steps. But we were stopped short when we heard what sounded like a muffled voice emanating from above. "What was that?" we asked each other in astonishment. "How could anyone be living here?" I wondered. Our curiosity aroused, we swallowed our fears and turned around to go check out the situation.

As we approached the next floor, the voice became more audible. "Uh, lets see," we heard a man muttering, "gotta get some milk and go to the post office, well maybe I should go first to the post office and then . . . ." As we got closer, the stench became stronger. We proceeded despite our revulsion until finally we were face to face with a man who looked and smelled as though he hadn't taken a shower in years. He didn't notice us and continued to mutter under his breath as he prepared for his errand.

"Hello, my name is Barry," said my companion, trying to establish contact. But the man continued to talk to himself, oblivious to our presence.

Barry and I were incredulous that he had been able to survive in these squalid conditions. We were even more surprised, though, when we heard a voice from one of the back rooms calling out the name "Fred." "Who's that?" we asked. He turned to walk away, and we asked if we could follow. He nodded.

Fear dissolved into concern and compassion as Barry and I passed the mounds of dust and heaps of garbage that led to the back recesses of the apartment. There we saw a woman lying in bed, under layers of covers. All that showed were her dark eyes. Just when we thought we had seen it all, the woman spoke up and said, "Poppa?" There, on the adjacent bed, under torn towels and army blankets, lay an ancient-looking man.

Barry and I tried to make sense of all this, but our rational minds could not comprehend what our eyes beheld. Our hearts weighed heavy as we gazed upon a state of humanity neither of us had known existed.

I leaned over to one bed and asked the woman her name.

"Dorothy," she responded, in a faint voice.

Barry and I explained to her why we were there and inquired about their situation. We learned that the elderly man was the father. Dorothy and the younger man, Fred, were sister and brother.

"What about your mother?" we inquired.

"She passed away a few years ago" was Dorothy's response.

"We would like to help you," Barry said. "Is that all right with you?" Dorothy nodded but wouldn't say much more.

We tried to find out how they had been able to sustain themselves and persevere in these conditions. It proved to be very difficult to obtain answers. The father appeared to be too weak to converse. Dorothy seemed lost in her thoughts. As for Fred, he was unable to engage in the simplest conversation.

Barry and I were utterly moved by this encounter and we vowed to help the family in any way we could. Over the next few months, Barry used all his contacts to help them. As a result of his efforts, the father was placed in a nursing home. The daughter, Dorothy, received treatment from an outpatient mental health facility, where she was placed on antidepressant medication. This enabled her to hold down a job that Barry was instrumental in obtaining for her. Both Dorothy and Fred were relocated to an apartment that was subsidized by the city. And Fred was placed under the care of a social service agency.

Standing in those squalid conditions on that autumn day, I promised myself that I would help those people in any way that I could. However, seeing that Barry was doing so much for them, I figured that there wasn't much more that I could contribute.

Twelve years later, their haunting image came to mind. I wondered about what had become of them and I pondered the many changes that had taken place since that time. As I sat in my office, I thought about Barry and recalled that he did indeed buy the building. For him, the deal worked out well. Our relationship though, did not. We were both fortunate to go on and find our respective mates and I had since become a psychiatric social worker. Memories came flashing back but were then interrupted when the door opened and the next patient walked in. And there he stood. The man I had vowed to help twelve years ago stepped right into my life.

I was one of thousands of social workers in the great metropolis. Fred counted as just one among the thousands of poor souls. "Will you help me?" he asked. He hadn't recognized me.

"Yes, Fred," I said, "I absolutely will." I became Fred's social worker and was able to fulfill the vow I had made long ago.

— *Judith Frankel Leventhal*

ઉ૯ ૱ૢૺ૦

Comment:

When you have a strong desire to perform an act of kindness, the universe assists in mysterious ways.

A *Queens*, New York woman leaned out of her eighth-floor tenement window and screamed for help. She was trapped in her bathroom. The inside knob had fallen off when her youngest child, age two, had closed the door from the other side. Two of her other children, ages four and five, were in the kitchen, alone, as supper cooked on the stove. The woman alternated between trying to break down the door herself and shouting to be heard. Both courses seemed futile and she was beginning to give up hope.

Meanwhile, a young man who lived twenty miles away happened to be visiting the neighborhood that day. From the street below, he heard the woman's pleas. He waved his hand to catch her attention and then screamed out, "I'm coming up to help you!" A short time later, she heard his voice from outside the bathroom door. "Listen closely," the young man instructed. "Put your fingers in the hole where the knob should be, pull it up, lift the door slightly, and then quickly pull it open." The woman followed the stranger's instructions, and within moments the door was open.

Once freed from her temporary prison, she ran to check on the children. In response to their mother's screams, they had become upset and needed some coddling to soothe their cries. When all three children were safe within her view, the woman turned to the young man and asked in amazement, "How could you possibly have known how to get into my apartment, and how did you know how that door opens?"

"I know very well," he answered with a smile crossing his face. "I was born here. I lived in this apartment for fifteen years. I know how to get in the front door without a key. And the bathroom knob? It would always fall off, and we learned to open the door just the way I showed you!"

༄

Comment:

Sometimes we need to walk back over routes we've already traveled in order to help someone cross a path we've crossed before.

*I*n his book *Journey to my Father*, Israel Zamir recounts how his father, Nobel laureate Isaac Bashevis Singer, frequently incorporated real-life material into his "fictional" works. Dramatic episodes and mysterious encounters that happened to friends, relatives, and neighbors eventually all worked their way into one of his mystical tales. Singer was often considered the master of the magical and the supernatural. Ironically, many of his most eerie stories were actually drawn from true life.

Zamir was in his father's house when the phone rang one day. The caller was an acquaintance of Singer's to whom a strange coincidence had just occurred. As the woman poured out her tale, Singer interrupted her remarks with repeated exclamations—"Really?" "Indeed?" "You're sure?"—shaking his head in amazement.

The woman caller, who lived on Long Island, had been out shopping and sometime during the day had lost the key to her apartment. It was her only key, she lived alone, and no one had a duplicate. Desperate, she wandered the streets for hours, hunting for the lost key. Retracing her steps, she returned to all the shops she had patronized that day and conducted thorough searches of the premises. Her tenacity, however, was not rewarded with success. As evening drew near, she decided to abandon her inquiries and travel to her sister's home in Brooklyn, where she would stay the night. She went to the local station of the Long Island Railroad to catch the next train. As she stood on line to buy a ticket, something on the floor next to the ticket booth—a shiny metal object—glinted and caught her attention. She bent down and picked up her key!

She had been nowhere near the train station that day, she told Singer, excitedly demanding an explanation from the man who filled his books with demons, sorcerers, and ghosts. His answer was that an "entity" had "made sure" that she would find what she was looking for, in order to protect her from having to travel to the wilds of Brooklyn at night! Finding the explanation perfectly acceptable, the woman thanked him and hung up.

The tale was avidly digested by Singer and became the basis for his story "The Key."

*C*oincidences don't happen only to adults. They can happen to children, too.

Just recently, my nine-year-old son reported the following story to me, in a tone filled with awe at the marvels and mysteries of the universe. "Last Thursday in school," he said, "I ate my snack during morning recess and it was salty, so I got very thirsty. We have a soda machine in the hallway and I wanted to buy a soda. But I was worried that recess might be over, so I asked a kid what time it was. 'It's 11:05 exactly,' he told me. I had five minutes to spare, so I ran down the hall to the machine. I have a habit of looking at each quarter before I put it into the machine, because I'm always hoping that somehow I'll get an old one that's worth a lot of money. So, as usual, I looked at each quarter before I inserted it. My teacher is very strict and gets very angry when we come into class late. I was so afraid that I was going to miss the recess bell that I made a mistake and put in an extra quarter. I put in four quarters instead of three. When I looked at the last quarter, I saw that the date written on it was 1980. I also saw a nick that I had made on that quarter during class, when I played with it and scratched a nickel across its surface. As soon as I put in the fourth quarter, I realized my mistake. I pressed the coin return and banged on the machine, but the only thing that came out was the Sprite. I noticed the principal walking by and asked him if I could get my lost quarter back.

"'Yeah, yeah, sure, sure,' he said absentmindedly. I could tell he didn't think my lost quarter was important. I ran back to class and later that day I went over to the principal again and asked for my quarter back a second time. 'Soon, soon,' he said. He seemed impatient. All week long, I asked him for my quarter and all week long, he repeated 'soon, soon.' But he never gave it back to me.

"Exactly one week later, also on a Thursday," my son told me, excitement rising in his voice, "during the first morning recess, I again wanted to buy a Sprite from the soda machine. Again, I was nervous about being late, so I asked a kid for the time. 'It's ll:05,' he said, 'exactly.' This time, I was very careful to be sure to put in only three quarters. I put in the three quarters and out came a Sprite. I was about to race down the hall to my class when I heard something drop into the coin return slot. I put in my fingers and pulled out a quarter. That's strange, I thought. So I looked at the quarter closely. It was dated 1980 . . . and it had a nick on it. It was *my* quarter . . . the exact same quarter I had lost the week before in the machine . . . at the exact same time . . . on the exact same day of the week. Can you imagine that!"

"So what do you think all of this means?" I asked my son, curious to hear his interpretation.

"Hey, mom," he said with a wide grin, "this lesson's easy to figure out!"

"Really," I said, bemused, "and what exactly is the lesson here?"

"When it's coming to you . . . it's coming to you!" he yelled exuberantly, triumph glinting in his eyes.

— *Yitta Halberstam Mandelbaum*

Comment

What a blessing for my son that, through the coincidence, he fortuitously learned that justice *is* indeed served in this world. Obviously losing a quarter is not a major tragedy, but still he might have come away from the experience a bit soured on the universe's sense of fair play. Perhaps, on a small scale, this experience might have given rise to a child's speculation that God cheats little kids. But given the startling symmetry between the two events, he came away with the perception that just the opposite holds true.

*O*n a cold day in 1942, inside a Nazi concentration camp, a lone young boy looks beyond the barbed wire and sees a young girl pass by. She too, is moved by his presence. In an effort to give expression to her feelings, she throws a red apple over the fence — a sign of life, hope, and love. The young boy bends over, picks up the apple. A ray of light has pierced his darkness.

The following day, thinking he is crazy for even entertaining the notion of seeing this young girl again, he looks out beyond the fence, hoping. On the other side of the barbed wire, the young girl yearns to see again this tragic figure who moves her so. She comes prepared with apple in hand. Despite another day of wintry blizzards and chilling air, two hearts are warmed once again as the apple passes over the barbed wire. The scene is repeated for several days. The two young spirits on opposite sides of the fence look forward to seeing each other, if only for a moment and if only to exchange a few words. The interaction is always accompanied by an exchange of inexplicably heartening feelings.

At the last of these momentary meetings, the young boy greets his sweet friend with a frown and says, "Tomorrow, don't bring me an apple, I will not be here.

They are sending me to another camp." The young boy walks away, too heartbroken to look back.

From that day forward, the calming image of the sweet girl would appear to him in moments of anguish. Her eyes, her words, her thoughtfulness, her red apple, all were a recurring vision that would break his nighttime sweats. His family died in the war. The life he had known had all but vanished, but this one memory remained alive and gave him hope.

In 1957 in the United States, two adults, both immigrants, are set up on a blind date. "And where were you during the war?" inquires the woman.

"I was in a concentration camp in Germany," the man replies.

"I remember I used to throw apples over the fence to a boy who was in a concentration camp," she recalls.

With a feeling of shock, the man speaks. "And did that boy say to you one day, 'Don't bring an apple anymore because I am being sent to another camp'?" "Why, yes," she responds, "but how could you possibly know that?"

He looks into her eyes and says, "I was that young boy."

There is a brief silence, and then he continues, "I was separated from you then, and I don't ever want to be without you again. Will you marry me?" They embrace one another as she says, "Yes."

On Valentine's Day 1996, on a national telecast of the *Oprah Winfrey* show, this same man affirmed his enduring love to his wife of forty years. "You fed me in the concentration camp," he said, "you fed me throughout all these years; now, I remain hungry if only for your love."

❦

Comment:
The darkest moments of one's life may carry the seeds of the brightest tomorrow.

In 1939, Japanese diplomat Chiune Sugihara, who was stationed in Lithuania during one of the darkest times in human history, saved thousands of Polish Jews from the Nazis by issuing transit visas to them. Defying his own government, he wrote visas day and night, even scribbling them by hand and passing them through a train window as he departed Lithuania.

His bold and extraordinary act of heroism was largely unknown and unsung in the immediate aftermath of the war. For many years he occupied an obscure footnote in history—until survivors who had been rescued by Sugihara began to emerge from the silence of their post-Holocaust shock and started telling his story. Soon, his courage and greatness were being celebrated all over the world, catching the attention of the mass media and inspiring several authors to write books describing the actions of the "Japanese Schindler."

Meanwhile, the Israeli government was gathering names of "courageous rescuers," whose efforts it wished to repay. One of the ways the Jewish state attempted to acknowledge its debt was by giving rescuers and their families sanctuary and lifelong pensions. Another, more symbolic way, was by planting trees in their honor. When Sugihara's valor came to light, Israeli officials immediately made plans to plant a cherry grove, as was customary, in his memory. But suddenly, in an uncommon move, officials rescinded the order. They decided that, in keeping with the breathtaking scope of Sugihara's actions, cherry trees were an inappropriate symbol. They opted instead for a grove of cedar trees, deciding that cedar was sturdier and had holier connotations, having been used in the First Temple.

It was only after they had planted the trees that the astonished officials learned for the first time that "Sugihara" in Japanese means . . . cedar grove.

Comment

Does a name confer a certain destiny? Is our fate formed by the name we are given at birth? While many people scoff at this concept, there are others who are quite careful, indeed even fanatical, about the names they select for their offspring, believing that sufficient evidence exists to strongly suggest just such a link.

In 1995, Susie Henderson* was forty-five, had never been married, and was stuck in a dead-end job. Dispirited as well by the failure of traditional psychotherapy to create meaningful change in her personal life, she decided to terminate her longstanding relationship with her psychologist and explore other, more unconventional avenues of help. She enrolled in a "personal growth" weekend series, took up meditation, prayed, studied at New Age retreat centers, even consulted with a psychic or two.

None of these brought the metamorphosis she hoped for, until she was directed by a friend to a "spiritual counselor" who incorporated "spiritual principles" into the psychotherapeutic process. Now, Susie finally began to experience the personal transformation she was seeking. She encountered fewer difficulties with men, formed more stable relationships with them, and was finally able to break free of the shackles that were binding her to a stifling job.

One of the techniques that Susie's spiritual counselor successfully taught her was to ask the universe for whatever it was she *truly* wanted. In session, Susie had often complained that God had failed to meet her needs.

Her therapist had stopped her short: "Well, did you ever really *ask*?"

"What do you mean, ask?"

"The universe is abundant and plentiful," the therapist had replied. "You simply have to ask God for what you want. But there is a technique to it." The therapist taught Susie the art of affirmation-making and stressed that one had to be extremely specific when articulating one's request. One had to tell God exactly what one wanted, and precisely when, how much, and for what purpose. Initially skeptical, Susie discovered to her own surprise that most of the time, asking God for what she wanted . . . worked.

One day, in her new job as residence manager of a home for the developmentally disabled, Susie was conducting a "goal-setting session" with the counselors on her staff. They were enormously overtaxed by the tremendous stresses of working with the profoundly dysfunctional and, using the session as a vehicle with which to let off steam, were complaining vigorously. Susie went around the room and, replicating the stratagems her own therapist had taught her, coached the counselors on how to achieve their goals. Although they ridiculed the exercise, Susie asked them to suspend their disbelief.

"Let's discuss what you would like to alter in your work environment," Susie began. "What changes could possibly increase your job satisfaction? What would *you* like to see happen? If you had a magic wand, what new scenarios would you want to create?" she challenged Denise, a sullen and disgruntled employee.

"What would I like to see happen?" shouted Denise, glad to have a chance to vent her rage and frustration. "Well, I am so damn tired of watching one of my patients, poor Karen, wait at the window day after day for relatives who never show up. No one in her family comes to visit. Her mother hasn't been here in six months. It breaks my heart . . . I can't take her pain anymore!"

"Okay," Susie said, nodding encouragingly. "So what exactly do you want?"

"I want her relatives to come visit, damn it!"

"Fine, let's articulate this wish in precise terms," Susie coached.

Susie worked with Denise for a few minutes, until Denise was able to stand up in the middle of the room and articulate her wish in the language of Susie's therapist: "I hereby make a commitment that Karen's mother and other relatives will come to visit her more often."

"*How often*?" Susie drilled. "You have to be precise."

Denise restated her request. "I hereby determine that her mother will come every two months."

"Perfect!" clapped Susie. "Okay. Now let's see what happens."

The very next evening, Karen's mother showed up at the home for the first time in six months. Susie's eyes sparkled when Denise told her the news. "Why do you think she came?" Susie asked.

"Uhh . . . someone probably called her to come," Denise mumbled in disbelief.

"Go ask her if that's what brought her here tonight," Susie directed.

But when confronted with the question, Karen's mother shook her head emphatically. "No, no one called me. I just happened to be in the neighborhood and decided to drop in."

Two days later, Karen's grandmother, who hadn't come to visit in four years, put in an appearance. "Did somebody call you to come?" Denise asked, startled to see her.

"No," said the grandmother. "I just started thinking about Karen, that's all. Something . . . I don't remember what . . . made me think of her."

The next day, Karen's aunt came and the day after that, her first cousin. "My God," said Denise to Susie, as a whole procession of relatives began to parade through the home to Karen's room. "Karen's had more visitors in one week than she's had all year!"

"So, what do you make of it?" Susie asked with a smile.

"Oh, it's very clear to me," Denise said with utmost certitude. "It's a . . . coincidence!"

<hr/>

Comment

This story vividly portrays the power of belief and its reverberations . . . on two entirely different levels. On one level, we have the dawning spiritual consciousness that our beliefs create our realities—the lesson that Susie's spiritual therapist taught, and that she in turn transferred to her staff. On another level, we learn from Denise's reaction the essential truth that basically most of us see what we want to see in life, and that ultimately the eye sees from the heart.

*W*hen Jimmy Haggerty* lived in New York, he won the state's ten-million-dollar lottery. Then he moved to New Jersey, where he collected an impressive eighteen million as the solitary winner in that week's draw. Then he moved to California, where for the third time in a row, he beat the odds, collecting twenty million from that state's lottery. When reporters frantically descended on him to interview him about these amazing coincidences, he shrugged his shoulders and said nonchalantly, "I didn't need to win any of them. I was wealthy from the start."

Comment

In a society driven by the work ethic, we sometimes find it hard to concede that a major component of success is sheer "luck" or "divine providence." In a way, though, it's a relief to accept that there's just so much we can do, and the rest is up to God.

*L*inda Valentine* was a famous model. Yet despite her money, fame, and glamour, she felt a gnawing emptiness inside. There was a sense of unease she could not cast off, a restlessness of spirit that filled her with unspeakable anxiety and dread. At night, she was plagued with insomnia. She began to ask her friends what they thought of taking prescription drugs like Xanax and Valium.

While many of them obligingly described the relative merits of each, one friend looked at Linda with genuine concern and took her aside. "That's not what you need," she whispered in distress. "Popping pills will only do you harm. And they only mask the symptoms, they don't address them. Are you free this weekend?"

That weekend, Linda's friend took her to a program called "Impact" that promised to help participants articulate and accomplish their goals. It delivered. Incredibly, within a short week of taking the seminar, Linda achieved career breakthroughs and won contracts she had been dreaming about for years. But despite the sudden fulfillment of her greatest ambitions, her general angst lingered. Her soul remained in torment.

One morning, she was taking her usual route to work, driving down La Brea, the main thoroughfare, when traffic came to a standstill. A water main had broken, and traffic was being diverted to a small, obscure street, one that she had never driven down before. As she inched her car along the unfamiliar street, she noticed a small storefront church with a handwritten sign in its window that proclaimed: "No God, no peace. Know God, know peace. Everybody welcome." "Hmm," she thought, as she drove slowly by, "how quaint!"

The next morning, Linda was on her way to work again, driving down La Brea, when, for the second day in a row, traffic came to a halt. A fire was blazing out of control in one of the shops lining the boulevard, and fire trucks were converging on the scene from all directions. Policemen blocked off the area, and diverted traffic to the same obscure street as the day before. "Oh, no!" she groaned, "not again!" Once again she drove by the small storefront church. This time, the sign seemed compelling, not quaint. She thought for a moment that it was summoning her inside. "What an imagination I have!" she laughed, scolding herself for her penchant for melodrama. Still, from her car window, she squinted at the storefront church, trying to catch a glimpse of its interior. Her gaze was wistful.

The next day, she thought of changing routes, but told herself that she was being foolish. After all, what were the odds of another calamity occurring on the same street three days in a row? "This will be a test," she chuckled to herself. "If there's some disaster on La Brea again, and traffic gets diverted down that same street again, then I'll know for sure it's a sign!"

When she turned down La Brea, she was thunderstruck. Traffic was backed up for blocks. A major car accident, explained an apologetic cop, diverting traffic again, for the third time in a row, down the same small street. "That does it!" she exclaimed. She parked her car and entered the church, which was empty except for a young priest sitting behind a desk. He looked up at her and smiled. "What took you so long?" he asked.

He had seen her car pass by all three days, and had absorbed her wistful gaze. They spoke for a long time, and she joined the congregation. That was eighteen years ago, and she's been there ever since, having found the peace and serenity that had eluded her elsewhere. Just as the sign promised, what she had really needed in her life was God. And wasn't it, after all, God who had sent her there in the first place?

Taylor Caldwell was a bestselling author in the 1950s and 1960s. For decades, her historical romances had dominated the bestseller charts. In terms of sales and excitement, she was the midcentury's equivalent of Danielle Steel.

Her devoted husband, with whom she had a long and wonderful marriage, preceded her in death. His death came after a protracted illness, and both had prepared for it. Just minutes before his death, Taylor Caldwell clutched her husband's hand and pleaded, "If there *is* life on the other side, I beg you, send me a sign. Let me know you are with me."

Her husband nodded his assent.

"Promise?" she begged.

"I promise," he pledged.

The next morning, overcome by her grief, Taylor Caldwell stepped out into her garden, seeking solace from nature as she always did. "Oh, darling," she cried out to her husband, "if you would only send me a sign that you are with me, I could try to go on. My pain is so wrenching and my grief so strong, I fear I cannot survive otherwise."

Just then, Ms. Caldwell approached a section of her garden where the ground had always proven stubbornly infertile and had never flourished like the surrounding area. As her gaze absently swept over this section, she gasped.

In the center of this section stood a rosemary bush that had not been productive for thirty years. Just the day before, when she had walked these same grounds seeking respite from her death watch, she had commented to herself how sorry she was that the bush had never thrived. But one day later, it was inexplicably in full bloom. Staring in shock and awe at the bush, Taylor Caldwell stood motionless for a long time, absorbing its message. "Thank you," she whispered fervently, "thank you. I will be able to go on, now that I know you are with me."

She had clearly been given the sign she was seeking, she told interviewers later. "You see," she explained, "rosemary means . . . remembrance."

Comment

When love is strong and runs deep, it pulsates with an energy that cannot be stopped, not even by death's grip. When two souls are connected and one departs from this world, the separation may seem final, but in truth the relationship transcends time. Love, like a river, flows eternal, and it embraces all those who swim in its streams.

*B*rooklyn College issues photo ID cards to all its students, which they must show to security guards at the entrances to various buildings on campus. Thus, I was utterly dismayed one evening when, at the entrance to the library, I reached into my wallet for my ID card, and discovered to my shock that it wasn't there! Although I begged the guard at the door to let me in because I had a paper due that required extensive research, my pleas fell on deaf ears and I was turned away. Fuming, I berated myself for having lost the ID card, and wondered how and where it had gone astray. I seemed to recall having taken my wallet out of my pocketbook sometime during the day, probably en route to work in Manhattan, but after that I drew a blank. I was annoyed at myself, because the process of applying for a new card was a bureaucratic nightmare, with hours of waiting on line for the application, for the photograph to be taken, for the ID card to be validated, etc. Worst of all, since the semester was already underway, the offices where I would need to go for help were only open during the daytime. I was an evening student and worked full-time. I would have to take a day off from work, and I had just started a new job.

I returned home later that night, still in a bad mood, still chastising myself, still wondering how I would approach my supervisor about a day off. As I walked through the door, the phone rang. It was my best friend, Toby.

"Guess what I found today at a subway station in Manhattan?" she crowed. "You're going to get a kick out of this!"

"Oh yeah, what?" I asked, uninterested, grumpy, and still obsessing.

"Your ID card!"

"What!" I screamed. "That's incredible! Where'd you find it?"

"At the Thirty-fourth Street station of the B train. I saw a piece of paper lying on the floor, and something just made me bend down and pick it up. Imagine my astonishment when I saw that—of all things—it's my best friend's picture!"

We both agreed that her retrieval of my ID card had been a minor miracle, and chalked it up to one of life's undeniable mysteries.

Just as she was about to hang up, I suddenly had a thought. "Toby . . . wait a second . . . it just dawned on me . . . You don't usually take the B train to Manhattan, do you?"

"No," she said, "but there was some mechanical trouble on the N train that I was originally on, and it was taken out of service. I waited around for another one, but when twenty minutes had passed and there was still no train in sight, I got frustrated and lost patience. So I walked through the station to switch to the B."

"Toby, do you realize," I said excitedly, "that if you had waited for the N train you would never have found my card?"

— *Yitta Halberstam Mandelbaum*

Comment

A missed plane that crashes . . . an object that mysteriously finds its way back to its owner . . . a friend's unexpected phone call precisely at the moment when we're undergoing a crisis or feeling especially blue. These are whispers that can awaken us from our stupor and remind us that the hand of God is always there, guiding us through our days.

*M*y mother, a widow, is practically destitute, and relies on me for financial help all the time. As I am not particularly well-off myself, this represents a tremendous pressure. Most of the time, I seem to be able to bear this burden with equanimity and good humor, but every now and then, the strain wears me thin. Such was the case last month, when my mother's air conditioner went on the blink during the worst heat wave of the summer.

For the preceding few months, she had been particularly needy. There had been unusual expenses to carry, in addition to the regular ones. Doctors' bills, summer clothes, a brief trip to the seashore . . . It seemed as though no day had passed that she hadn't called me about a new bill she wanted me to pay. So when she called and told me she needed a new air conditioner, I snapped. "Not now!" I screamed, slamming down the phone hard.

That night, I came home late from work, and found that my apartment resembled a steam bath. As soon as I opened the door, the hot air hit me instantly, and beads of sweat began pouring down my face and body. "Thank God I have central air conditioning!" I said to myself, as I moved the dial on the meter to turn it on.

I waited for the cold air to come pouring through the vents, but nothing happened. I suddenly realized that the slow, steady vibrating hum that always signified the functioning of the central air conditioner was missing. "I can't believe it!" I muttered to myself in dismay. "The central air conditioner—which has never given me a minute's trouble—is broken . . . on the hottest night of the year!"

It was eleven o'clock at night and too late to call a repairman. I would literally have to sweat it out till the next morning.

I was so uncomfortable that night that I couldn't sleep. I tossed and turned, showered repeatedly, gulped down cold drinks. But nothing helped. It was unbearably hot outside, and I was in misery.

Suddenly, I sat up in bed. "Oh my God!" I thought guiltily. "My poor mother! If I, a healthy forty-year-old, am experiencing such tremendous discomfort, what is she going through? How could I have been so insensitive, so uncaring?"

I felt overwhelmed with shame and remorse at my callous behavior the day before, at my lack of compassion for my mother. But perhaps I was not entirely to blame. Perhaps I had not really understood how oppressive the heat could be. I had finally gotten a glimmer of what she had been experiencing when my own air conditioning broke down. "First thing in the morning I'm going to buy her an air conditioner!" I immediately resolved. "I won't even go to work until I make sure the air conditioner is installed in her bedroom. No, better yet, I'm not going to buy her one air conditioner . . . I'm going to buy her one for every room in the house!"

Satisfied with my envisioned act of expiation, I settled back into my pillows and closed my eyes. Suddenly, I heard the most welcome noise in the world: the whir of the air conditioning motors and a reassuring hum.

Cold air blasted through the vents. I gasped in wonderment and disbelief at the impeccable timing. And then I knew: my penance had been accepted.

— *Celia Robbins* *

Comment

We think that concrete physical actions are the only possible manifestations of our benevolence. But in fact, just the *thought* of doing a good deed is powerful enough to effect a change in the universe.

*F*or years, my family had made a tradition of traveling to the Pine View Hotel in the Catskill Mountains every spring for the Passover holidays. We had been doing this for over ten years, and during this time had made many close friends with other "repeats." My parents had become especially close to a lovely couple from out-of-state who were also frequent guests at this popular resort. Although they didn't keep in touch with one another over the course of the year, when they did meet at the Pine View, they all shared an unusual camaraderie.

By now, my parents had known this couple — Eve and David Stern* — for over a decade and considered them one of the most happily married couples they had ever met. They looked forward to their yearly reunions. Thus, one Passover, as my parents were checking in at the registration desk, they were shocked to encounter Eve standing in the lobby, clinging to the arm of a different man, whom she immediately introduced as "my new husband." My parents nearly fainted.

As soon as she could, my mother drew Eve aside and asked what had happened over the last year. Eve shrugged her shoulders in a parody of bewilderment and said that, to tell the truth, she was as astonished as my mother about the unusual series of events that had

151

occurred. She herself was still reeling, she said, from the peculiar twists of fate she had experienced in recent months. She didn't know what to make of it all, she told my mother, but she would gladly recount the sequence of events that defied reason.

"About eleven months ago," she related, "my husband stormed into my room one day and dropped a bombshell into my lap. He told me, without any explanation or apology whatsoever, that he wanted a divorce. I was stunned. I had always been quite content in our marriage, and I assumed he was too. There had never been any previous difficulties, and no plausible cause for his sudden outburst. As much as I tried to beg him for a reason, a motive, a basis for his abrupt request, he wouldn't give me any. He insisted that he had always been unhappy, and wanted to make a change in his life now before it was too late. I was devastated and heartbroken, but after several weeks of trying to get him into counseling or change his mind, I succumbed. I had my pride; I didn't want to live with someone who didn't want to live with me. So I gave him the divorce, and we went our separate ways.

"Six months later, I met and married the man whom I introduced to you in the lobby. He's a wonderful man, and I'm deliriously happy. In fact, I'm much happier than I was in my first marriage. Everything has gone exceptionally well.

"There's only one jarring note," Eve said slowly. "One thing that kind of gives me the willies, and for which I can find no possible rational explanation.

"You see, my second husband is also named David Stern—same as the first. Well, you could argue that both the first name David and the surname Stern are fairly common, so that's not what gives me the creeps. What I do find eerie is that both my second and my first husband were born on the exact same day, month, and year. They were both born on September 8, 1931.

"Now, how," she said, turning to my mother, "do you explain that?"

— *Shira Freedman*

Comment

There are markers that set us on a course for life. We are born under a certain star and we are given a specific name. These point us in a direction that we may not understand. For often it is too difficult to step back from ourselves and gain enough distance to see how the markers all play out in the greater scheme of our lives.

*W*hen Miri Fabian, an Israeli stage actress, won a small role in Steven Spielberg's film *Schindler's List*, she felt mixed emotions. "I had auditioned on videotape," she recalls, "and didn't know what it was for—only that it was for Spielberg. I had seen *The Color Purple* and *Empire of the Sun*. Then I found out I got the part and what it was. I was happy but also very sad. I had been born in a Slovakian work camp in 1944 and was cast as one of the women saved by Schindler. Here was something my mother had saved me from—Auschwitz—and here I was going back of my own free will. It was poignant.

"To help me prepare for the part, I was given the name and number of the daughter of the character I was playing and called her. When I phoned, I said, 'I'm playing your mother in *Schindler's List* and would like to know everything about her. Can I visit you?' I did, and the daughter graciously showed me old photographs of her mother as she had looked then and current photographs as she looks today.

"I practically leaped to my feet in astonishment. 'But I know your mother!' I shouted. 'She lives in the house opposite me. I see her every day on the street!'"

*D*ear Abby,

Several weeks ago, you asked readers to share their experiences of suicide attempts that failed or were aborted. I know you've already printed many, so I hope you don't mind printing one more.

Ten years ago, everything hit me from all sides. I became depressed and suicidal. I attempted to kill myself once in a motel, but a cleaning lady saved me.

I came out of the hospital still determined to end my life. I began saving prescription pills. When I went to church in search of answers, I would look around to see if there was a way I might hang myself from the ceiling. Two months later, I tried again. I headed for a small town and took 300 prescription pills with me.

A friend traced me to the motel. Three other friends talked me into going to the hospital. I walked into that hospital with the 300 pills, determined to kill myself there.

While seated in the lobby, I picked up a *Reader's Digest* and randomly opened it without looking at the index. Here is the unbelievable part: The page I arbitrarily turned to contained an article entitled *Before You Kill Yourself.* It gave several powerful reasons to choose life over suicide.

I called a nurse and handed her all the pills I had hidden. You should have seen her face!

That *Reader's Digest* article saved my life. That was ten years ago, and I am doing just fine now!

— From a September 1995 column

❧

Comment

Sometimes all that may be needed to salvage the soul and mend the heart is a kind word and a message of hope and inspiration.

Gerry drove a big red Cadillac. It served as a multipurpose vehicle. On weekends, the whole family enjoyed the use of the car, and during the week, Gerry used it to cart his wares. Gerry was a salesman and he kept samples of his electronic merchandise in the car's trunk.

A typical workday for Gerry involved making various sales calls at different locations. On August 15, 1994, Gerry made a stop at Bob's Electronics, with the hope of making a substantial sale. Through the store window, he was able to see Bob, the storeowner, walking to the cash register. Rather than parking the car for what he assumed would be a two-minute exchange, Gerry left the engine running as he walked up to the store. "Hey, Bob!" Gerry called while holding the door ajar, "need anything?"

"Not today, Gerry," came the reply. "But try me again at the end of the week."

"Will do," said Gerry, and headed quickly back toward the car.

But there was no car. That two-minute exchange had given someone ample time to get behind the wheel and drive off. Gerry was aghast. First, he called the police, and then he called his good friend Mike. "Mike!" he cried into the phone, "they got my Cadillac!"

"What do you mean?" asked Mike.

"What do I mean?!? I mean MY CAR WAS STOLEN!!" yelled Gerry.

Mike was concerned. "Where are you?" he asked. "I'll come right over."

Gerry gave him the address and then waited anxiously for help.

The police were the first to show up. Moments later, Mike arrived. The police took down all the necessary information and assured Gerry that all efforts would be made to retrieve his car. Having completed their preliminary work, they left.

Mike turned to Gerry and in an overly optimistic tone, said, "C'mon, let's go look for your car ourselves."

Gerry was incredulous. "The thief might be anywhere by now!" he barked, "Brooklyn is a VERY BIG PLACE! Where would we possibly begin to look?"

"I guess you're right," responded Mike, his spirit dampened. "It *is* a ridiculous idea. Listen," he went on, "I need to buy a pair of pliers from Rickel's Home Center. Think you can wait in the car for me while I run in and get it? It'll just be a minute."

"No problem," said Gerry. He was feeling extremely down on his luck and welcomed the opportunity to be with his close buddy, regardless of where they were going or what they were doing.

Twenty minutes later they arrived at Rickel's massive parking lot. "I don't think I'm in the mood to go inside," said Gerry. "Let me wait out here for you."

"All right with me," responded Mike as he left the car. "Like I said, it'll only take a few minutes."

Gerry sat slumped in the seat, looking out at all the hundreds of cars in the parking lot. It was a hazy day. The gray clouds mirrored his gray mood. Suddenly, for a fraction of a second, the clouds parted and a strange light shone from the sky.

Gerry was mesmerized by this single ray, which was shining on one car. It was as though a laser beam had pierced through the clouds and settled on this one automobile. "How strange," thought Gerry. He craned his head out the window to take a better look at the ray of sunshine dancing on the hood of the car. Then his head shot up. It was *his* car.

Parked among the thousands of cars in the vast parking lot was his very own red Cadillac. Gerry called the police again. This time it was to reclaim his property.

A *certain* homeless man who walked the streets of our neighborhood had become a fixture in our household over the years. My husband, Good Samaritan that he was, had seen "Bert" scavenging in our garbage cans one day, and stopped to speak with him. Learning that he was homeless, he took pity on him, and invited him inside for a hot meal. Since he was dressed neatly, and spoke in educated, well-modulated tones, I never suspected a thing. His breadth of knowledge was far-ranging and extensive, and during dinner he regaled us with intelligent and witty comments about politics, medicine, and urban affairs. My husband had deliberately refrained from telling me Bert's background, and by the time dinner was over and the truth was out, my prejudices about "street people" were shattered forever.

Bert was in and out of our lives over the course of the next fifteen years. I learned that he held a master's in physics from City College and had experienced a nervous breakdown in his twenties after his mother, father, and fiancée all died within a three-month period. At first I tried to help Bert. I spoke earnestly to officials at several social service agencies about trying to enroll him in welfare, getting him an apartment or at least a room, and finding him a job. I even made arrangements with a local senior citizens' center to give Bert a free hot lunch every day. But he never kept a single one of the appointments I excitedly but naively made for him — never even put in an appearance at the senior citizens' center, where all that was required of him was that he show up. Eventually I gave up. There was something wizardlike, secretive, and hidden about him, and it seemed as though he possessed a mysterious past that he was trying hard to conceal. In time, I began to accept Bert for what he was. I always opened our home to him and shared our meals with him, giving him cash and clothing whenever I had some to spare. But I no longer tried to change his life.

Bert was pleasant company, jovial and witty, and I always marveled at his optimistic spirit. Despite his bleak circumstances, he seemed to be perpetually in a good mood. It was therefore never any kind of effort or sacrifice to have him around, even though my friends remarked constantly on my so-called "altruism."

After fifteen years of hosting Bert without incident, I was startled one day to receive a visit from a neighbor who said she had come to warn me about him. She couldn't help but notice his comings and goings, she said, and she wanted me to know that he was nothing but a common thief.

"How do you know this?" I demanded in disbelief.

"Haven't you ever noticed anything missing from your home?" she asked with a sly look.

"No, never," I replied. "Well, you're so absentminded to begin with, you probably wouldn't even be aware if something was stolen from under your nose!"

"Why are you saying these things?" I demanded. "On what basis?"

"I saw him in front of a local store the other day. The police were frisking him. He had stolen something from the shop. And the storeowner, whom I personally know, said that all the shopkeepers on the avenue have learned to be wary of him. He has a reputation for pilfering, and he's also said to be violent."

"Are you sure we're talking about the same man?" I insisted, incredulous and shaken.

"It's definitely the same man," the neighbor answered with certitude. "I'd recognize him anywhere. So I came to tell you . . . beware!"

That evening, the doorbell rang, and with a sinking heart, I looked out the window and saw that it was Bert. My husband had taken our two sons to a baseball game, and I was all alone. For the first time since I had met him, I was suddenly afraid of Bert and didn't want him in the house. I stuck my head out the second-story window and yelled, "Hi, Bert! How ya doing?" He squinted up at me, brows knitted in puzzlement. This was not part of our routine; usually, I just opened the door and warmly ushered him inside.

"Uhh, Yitta," he stammered, confused by the obvious shift, "can you open the door? I'm starving!"

I felt anguished. "Oh, Bert, I'm so sorry, I was just about to leave the house this minute for a doctor's appointment." "Well, do you think you could wait just a little bit while I eat? It's cold tonight and I sure could use a warm meal." I thought of the four pieces of chicken and the mashed potatoes on the stove waiting for my family's return. Ordinarily, I would have given Bert my portion without hesitation, but after the neighbor's visit, I found myself gripped by fear. The jovial man who had graced our table for years as a friend suddenly loomed as a stranger whom apparently I had never really known at all. "So sorry, Bert," I hedged. "Really, I have to leave this minute. But tell you what, I'll pack a shopping bag for you with stuff you can eat."

I raced around the kitchen, pulling out cheese, fruit, and hardboiled eggs from the fridge, crackers, sardines, seltzer, and paper goods from the pantry. When I opened the door and handed the bag to him, his face had a hurt and bewildered expression. I felt ashamed. "Well, thank you for this," he said gesturing towards the bag as he strode down the walkway. "But I sure could have used a hot meal tonight," he threw over his shoulder, before he disappeared.

As I waited for my husband and children to return home from the baseball game, I wrestled with tumultuous thoughts, besieged by self-doubt. "You did the right thing," comforted one voice. "What are you, crazy? — to let a thief into the house! Charity is one thing and stupidity is another."

"You were wrong to turn him away!" strongly rebuked another voice. "He's been in your home for fifteen years, and nothing ever happened. You let yourself be swayed by a vicious gossip. How can you know for sure it was really Bert she was talking about, anyway?"

On and on it went all evening, the verbal sparring between my two inner voices never ceasing, my despair, remorse, and guilt growing with each passing minute. Had I done the right thing? Had I been wrong? How would I ever know the truth?

Finally, my family came home from the baseball game starved, and I began to concentrate on serving dinner. Holding my husband's plate, I began walking towards the dining room table, when I stumbled over a toy on the floor. The plate crashed to the floor, and food flew in all directions. "Don't worry, I have plenty to go around," I lied, planning to give my husband my portion.

The second plate heaped with food had been safely navigated onto the table, when the phone rang. It was for my husband, and he left his place at the table to answer the call. When he returned to the dining room, he stared in astonishment at the sight of our beagle, Flash, perched on her hindquarters, gobbling up his food from the plate. She had been with the family for five years and had never done anything like this before. "Is there enough food to go around now?" he asked, scowling angrily at Flash. "Sure, sure," I lied, wondering how I was going to stretch the remaining pieces of chicken three ways. Just as I approached the stove a third time, the light bulb in the overhead hood inexplicably exploded, scattering shards of glass all over the burners and into the pot of food, which I had left uncovered. Hearing the pop of the exploding bulb, my husband came into the kitchen to investigate, and immediately flung the pot's contents into the garbage can. "Is our dinner jinxed tonight?" he joked good-naturedly.

I began to cry. "Why are you crying?" he chided. "It's not your fault."

"Oh, yes, it is," I sobbed, and I explained what had happened with Bert.

As my husband and boys left the house for the nearest restaurant, I thought of Bert, who didn't have that recourse, who didn't have hot food in his belly to keep him warm through the cold night.

Before the "coincidental" mishaps with the food had occurred that evening, I had wondered long and hard about whether I had done the right or wrong thing about Bert. Had I canvassed my friends for their opinions (which I typically do whenever I'm faced with a moral dilemma), I am sure the answers would have been conflicting, indeterminate, and confusing. Some friends would have reassured me that I was justified in closing both my house and heart to Bert, while others, I know, would have scolded me rigorously for listening to gossip and not giving Bert the benefit of the doubt. My soul-searching would have remained tormented, my quandary unresolved.

But attuned to the message of the mishaps, I knew that I had made a mistake. For in the coincidences, I had found the incontrovertible truth.

— *Yitta Halberstam Mandelbaum*

Comment:

The universe provides the answers to our questions. We can hear them if only we open our hearts and tune in our souls.

 *lanca* was born in Satmar, a small town on the outskirts of Hungary. She was the third in a family of ten—seven girls and three boys. As part of a large family and in a community bustling with children, Blanca was somewhat lost in the shuffle. She was not an exemplary student. She did not exhibit exceptional talent, nor was she especially popular with her friends. No one took particular notice of her.

No one except for Sergi.

He was a young boy who lived down the block. From the time that they were both very young, Blanca and Sergi played together in the courtyards of their homes and in the fields on the edge of town. Long after all the others had outgrown childlike games, they continued to delight in frivolous play. When he was fourteen years old, Sergi spoke to his mother about his plans for the future. "I'm going to marry Blanca one day," he said over dinner.

"Sure you will," replied his mother, and then encouraged him to finish his meal. Blanca knew how much Sergi cared about her, and it made her feel special.

Sergi's admiration for Blanca grew, as did the years. On the evening of her fifteenth birthday, Sergi came to celebrate. "Blanchuka!" he called to her from the back window of her house. Blanca peered out. There Sergi stood, serenading her with love songs, accompanied by a band of gypsies playing violins and guitars. "You are so special to me," he called up to her. "Sergica," she sighed. As Blanca leaned out the window, listening to Sergi sing, she felt cherished and loved.

For the two budding sweethearts, life was good but it didn't last too long. Shortly after their special night, World War II broke out. In anticipation of the worst, Blanca's parents prepared to move the family to America. Blanca was devasted. "How can I leave Sergi behind?" she thought. "But how can I not?" At fifteen years of age, Blanca did not imagine that she had any choice but to follow her parents' lead. "I will miss you," Blanca said to Sergi between tears.

"Write to me," Sergi implored. The two promised to stay in touch and meet again someday soon.

For Blanca, the move to America was difficult and unsettling. Though she longed to stay in touch with Sergi, the war made it impossible to do so. When Blanca turned eighteen, her parents arranged for her to meet a young man who had a fine reputation. Blanca's heart still yearned for Sergi, but she was persuaded to leave the past behind. She married the young man and together they raised a family of five. Despite various challenges, their marriage was good. As time wore on, the memory of Sergi faded somewhat but was never totally forgotten.

In 1995, Blanca returned to her homeland. She was now a grandmother of ten. She had heard from a distant relative that Sergi was still living in Satmar. This information awakened in her a desire to go back to her native land. She yearned to tell Sergi how much he had meant to her through the years. She wanted to tell him that he had remained a sweet memory, that she had never stopped loving him with the innocent love she had for him as a child.

Blanca walked the streets of Satmar, surprised by how small it seemed compared to the way she remembered it. She recalled that when she was a young girl, a horse and buggy was a familiar sight. Now taxis, buses, and cars were everywhere. She hailed a taxi. "Please," she said in her native tongue, "could you take me to this address?" Blanca showed the taxi driver the street name and number where Sergi reportedly lived.

"Ah, my dear friend Sergi," the taxi driver said, "you want to see him?"

"Why, yes," Blanca said, surprised that the driver knew him.

"You did not hear?" the taxi driver said in a lowered voice. "Why, yesterday, Sergi passed away."

Blanca never did get to say what was in her heart. Instead, she visited his cemetery plot, laid a wreath on his tombstone, kissed it gently, and walked away.

Comment

We think there is always a tomorrow, so why expose our feelings today? Why risk being vulnerable? Why take the chance? Because today, what we love, what we feel, what is real, is what we have. Tomorrow, it may all change.

Nature calls to me as I am walking down Lexington Avenue in New York City. I decide to do what I have always done, which is a version of the following: I saunter into an upscale restaurant. Typically I am stopped by the maitre d', who asks, "How may I help you?" I glibly reply, "Oh, I'm supposed to meet someone—do you mind if I look around to see if they are here?" An affirmative response always follows. "Sure, go ahead." I then pretend I am surveying the tables for a familiar face. When I am out of clear view of the maitre d', I find my way to the ladies' room and proceed to take advantage of the facilities. On the way out I mumble something to the maitre d' like, "Thanks, but I couldn't find the person I was looking for," and hastily exit.

That's the way it has always been. So one day, I proceed with my usual routine. I walk into an unfamiliar restaurant. I follow the usual protocol. I get as far as the bathroom, and then for some unknown reason, I am suddenly struck with pangs of guilt! My conscience decides to take a stand for honesty. Right there and then, in the bathroom, I begin having a major philosophical debate about the ethics of lying. "A lie to a total stranger doesn't count," I argue.

"A lie is a lie!" my conscience retorts.

After much deliberation, I decide that the truth must prevail and that I must repent. Then I hear a stern command from my superego: "Tell the maitre d' that you lied. Once you do that, you will have purged yourself of the wrongdoing you have committed and you will never, never do it again."

With my conscience in command and my morals high, I walk bravely over to the maitre d', steeling myself for a prickly situation. I clear my throat, readying myself to tell him that I really wasn't expecting to meet anyone. And then suddenly and unexpectedly, an old friend walks through the door, gives me a great big bear hug and says, loud enough for the maitre d' to hear, *"Hi! So glad to see you!"*

Just as I was about to lose respectability in a stranger's eyes, I was found by a friend who returned my dignity to me intact. As I left the restaurant, I looked over my shoulder and took note of its name. Appropriately enough, it was called "The Lost and Found."

Comment

The path of truth is paved with a light that burns through darkness and dispels shame.

abbi Abraham Leifer of Ashdod, Israel, who died five years ago, was a celebrated rabbi with many followers. When one of his faithful flock married off a child in Antwerp, Belgium, Rabbi Leifer took an entourage from Israel with him and flew to the wedding. They were nine men in all.

When they were only three hundred miles away from Antwerp, the pilot suddenly announced that the plane was low on fuel and they would have to make an unscheduled stop. They landed at a small country airport.

Everyone deplaned, and the rabbi and his followers decided to look for a solitary spot where they could conduct the evening prayer service. The rabbi approached an airport worker, and asked him if it would be possible to open up a room where they could pray privately. The request was couched in ordinary terms, in English, but the man blanched as if he had been punched. He stared at the rabbi in disbelief and then answered, "I'll grant your wish . . . provided that you allow me to chant the *kaddish* (the Jewish memorial prayer for the dead) for my father!"

"You are a Jew?" the rabbi asked in bewilderment. The man nodded yes. "I didn't know any Jews lived in this part of Belgium. What are you doing here?" The man rejoined, "Better yet . . . what are *you* doing here . . . today of all days, just when I need you?"

As the man opened the door of the private room the rabbi had requested, he said: "Let me tell you something, which you may find difficult to believe. But I promise it is true."

"I broke with my family years ago and fled to this small village. Although I originally come from an extremely Orthodox family, I myself have not been religious for decades. I have not said *kaddish* for my father in years.

"Last night, I had a dream in which my father came to me and said: 'Yankele, tomorrow is the anniversary of my death and I want you to say the *kaddish* for me!' 'But father,' I protested in the dream, 'you need a *minyan* (a quorum of ten men) in order to say kaddish. I'm the only Jew in this village. I can never hope to find a *minyan* here!' 'Yankele,' my father answered, 'if you promise me you'll say the *kaddish*, I promise you I'll bring you a *minyan*!'

"When I awoke from the dream," the man told my uncle, "I was trembling and in shock. But I soon told myself it was only a dream, and reassured myself that it had no significance. It was ridiculous, really! After all, how would a *minyan* ever find their way to a remote Belgian farming village where no other Jews reside?"

The rabbi draped his arm around the man's shoulders, and said gently, "Come my friend, let's pray!"

*I*n September 1995, my eight-year-old son came home from school one day to report excitedly that a new kid from overseas had just joined his class. This kid, he told me happily, "is just like me in every way. It's really cool, Mom," he said. "Josh loves basketball, he's great at sports, he's mischievous, he's funny, and he knows how to play great tricks on the teachers!" (Terrific! Now the poor souls would have to contend with a devilish duo instead of just one menace who had previously operated solo!) Sure enough the two fun-loving, spirited imps teamed up for a series of hijinks, innocent pranks, and frolicking escapades that had the school staff reeling. My son was ecstatic about his new friend. "It's amazing how much he's like me," he constantly commented, in a tone of wonderment and delighted surprise.

One day, my son came home with Josh to work on a school project together. Since he lived in a different neighborhood, Josh asked if I could drive him home when they were done, and I readily agreed. When I pulled up at his address, he asked if I would like to come in and meet his mother. The hour was late, but never one to rebuff a child, I obligingly climbed out of the car. Josh ushered me into the living room and went to find his mother. "Eli's mother is here!" I heard him call to her. "Come meet her . . . you'll love her!"

Quick, light footsteps danced down the stairs and I turned to meet Josh's mother. She blinked. I blinked. Her jaw dropped. My mouth gaped open. Her eyes filled with tears. I tried hard to muffle a sob. Then we simultaneously ran towards each other and embraced for a long time.

Josh stood staring at this scene transfixed and perplexed. "What's going on?" he asked.

"Oh, Josh!" his mother exclaimed laughing, wiping away a tear. "Eli's mother and I were best friends in high school. After graduation, I moved abroad and I met Dad and lived overseas for years. I haven't seen Yitta for twenty-two years!"

Of course, I hadn't had an inkling. How could I have known? It was his father's surname—"Goodfriend"—that Josh used, not his mother's maiden name, although perhaps, on second thought, the name should have provided me with a slight suspicion, if not a telltale clue!

— *Yitta Halberstam Mandelbaum*

Comment

The legacy of love and friendship spans and is transmitted by the generations, perhaps even genetically imprinted upon us in some mysterious and unfathomable way. Invisible lines of connection link us all, and the heart always returns to its source. Once attachments are formed, they never truly disappear, but continue to live on, in our thoughts, our deeds, and our children's lives.

*I*n the 1950s, when it was unacceptable for a woman of breeding to work, Eppie Lederer of Chicago was faced with a quandary: how to direct her dynamism and energy, and what to do about her growing restlessness.

She had one teenage child who was away in school all day, and a busy executive husband who traveled much of the time. Having relocated to the big city in 1954 from Eau Claire, Wisconsin, where she had been active in civic affairs, she thought of entering local politics but had been warned away. "The Chicago machine is not manned by La Follette Democrats, let alone women," an old friend cautioned. "If you try your hand at local politics, you just might wind up in Lake Michigan wearing a cement ankle bracelet."

"I have to do something," she thought. "I must have a calling!" She didn't know what it was, but surely she would know it when she found it.

In August 1955, Eppie was reading the *Chicago Sun-Times* when a certain feature captured her attention. She read the column over and over again, once, twice, three times, with mounting interest. It was the advice column, penned by a woman named Ann Landers. At the bottom of the column, there was a note encouraging people to send their problems to Ann Landers, with the promise that all letters would be personally answered, even if they weren't used in the paper. "That columnist must be swamped," thought Eppie. "I bet she could use an assistant. Now that's something I'd like to do: help Ann Landers answer her mail!"

She promptly picked up the phone and called an executive she knew at the paper. "I've figured out what I'd like to do," she announced to Will Munnecke. "I'll help Ann Landers answer her mail."

There was a long pause on the other end. "Now this is odd," said Munnecke, "that you should be calling me now. Ruth Crowley, our 'Ann Landers,' just died suddenly . . . I'll call you back."

But by the time Munnecke had returned her call, Eppie Lederer had already revised her plans: since there was no one to be an assistant *to*, she would simply take over the entire column herself!

She knew it was a reach, but she had a feel for this kind of thing, she told Munnecke. In response, the executive laughed. "My dear," he chuckled, "the newspaper business is not about granting wishes to ladies with sudden inspirations and nothing to do!" When he sensed that Eppie's feelings had been hurt, he tried to cushion the blow by gently explaining that this column called for training that she simply didn't have. Crowley had been both a newspaperwoman and a nurse. And there was the added complication that "Ann

Landers" wasn't just a local feature, but was syndicated in forty papers throughout the country.

But Eppie Lederer was not deterred. She asked how the new Ann Landers would be selected. "By competition," Munnecke answered. "All the contestants will be given the same letters so their answers can be compared for substance and style. Twenty-one contestants—most of them writers and reporters, a few of them executive's wives—have been lined up." "Well, now you have twenty-two!" answered Eppie feistily. Munnecke saw no point in arbitrarily keeping Eppie out of the contest. She would soon realize of her own accord that she couldn't cut it, he thought. "Fine, you're in the contest," he said.

Eppie Lederer had never written a line for publication, and had never held a paying job. But she had other qualifications that were important: common sense, motivation, energy, a clear idea of right and wrong—and tremendous self-confidence. The competition stretched over the course of many weeks and she kept knocking out sample columns that were entertaining, authoritative, and easy to understand. The judges at the *Sun-Times* were impressed—but they didn't know by whom, because each contestant had a code number. This bit of blind justice was necessitated by the presence of the executives' wives in the contest.

Week by week, more would-be Ann Landerses were eliminated, until the final decision was made. The numbers were decoded and the winner was . . . Eppie Lederer? There was a small meeting with Eppie and a few executives. They gave her a less-than-ringing vote of confidence.

"You'll never last," they said.

⸎

Comment:

This story teaches us the importance of acting on impulse and being spontaneous, rather than being restrained by logic and reason (which many of us seem to feel is the higher good). It's important to be able to simply seize the moment, and be mindful of opportunities when they present themselves.

*H*enry was pushing the speed limit, going northbound on Ocean Parkway in Brooklyn, New York. He was headed to a business meeting and he had no time to spare. His eyes darted around as he surveyed the other cars, and he quickly maneuvered his way through the traffic like a rattlesnake in the rocks. Just as Henry was about to enter the Brooklyn Queens Expressway, he was cut off by a vehicle turning in from the service road. Henry opened his window and bellowed out some hardcore profanities. Sam, the other driver didn't want to take that lying down. He was in a rush as well. So Sam put his anger into action and cut Henry off at the next turn. Henry's escalating tension now turned to anger at this nervy driver who had now ticked him off twice. Within seconds, Henry cut him off, leaving only inches between the two cars. The heat escalated as the two guys drove like manic daredevils. Just as Henry thought he had left the other car in a cloud of dust, he looked in the rearview mirror and there it was again. Sam stepped on the gas, opened his window, and matched Henry's profanities and then some. This only added fuel to the fire in Henry's eyes, and the chase took on an even more perilous angst.

But just as suddenly as it had all begun, it came to an abrupt, screeching halt. Henry stopped and got out of his car, and was surprised to see Sam pull up right alongside him. The two men marched right into the same building. Then into the same elevator. There were raised brows as they glared at one another. Both were utterly bewildered as they walked out of the elevator and through the same door.

The truth became apparent as they began to speak in civil tones: Henry the supplier and Sam the customer were running late to meet each other.

❧

Comment:

Be kind to the people you meet on the highways and byways of your life because paths cross, lanes merge, and you never know where or when you may meet some of those very same people once again.

In 1900, while writing his famous book on the atmosphere, the British astronomer Camille Flammarion was working on the chapter on wind force when a sudden, unnaturally strong gust of wind swept all his papers off the table and blew them out of the window. As they fluttered to the ground several yards away from his home, an acquaintance of Flammarion's walked by and saw the pile of papers heaped on the ground. Looking them over, he discerned immediately that they were Flammarion's work and assumed that he had dropped them on his way to his publisher's. Hoping to avert an alarm being raised for the missing chapter, the man decided to personally deliver it to the publishing house. The editor, however, was absent from his office (which boasted huge windows that were open at the time), so Flammarion's friend simply placed the chapter on his desk, without leaving a note of explanation. The next day, Flammarion was astonished to learn from the editor that he had in his possession the missing chapter, and both concluded with growing excitement that it must have been blown in by the wind—completely intact! It was only several days later that the friend would meet Flammarion and disabuse him of this dramatic notion.

Despite his disappointment with the more pedestrian truth, Flammarion's interest in the subject was piqued, and became heightened by another true story of coincidence that was recounted to him by a friend:

When he was a young boy in Orléans, France, a certain Monsieur Deschamps was once given a piece of plum pudding—an uncommon delicacy and luxurious tidbit—by a Monsieur de Fortgibu, a middle-aged neighbor. Delighted by the treat, the young boy ate it slowly and with relish, savoring every tasty morsel. He did not encounter this rarity again until ten years later, when he saw a lone plum pudding sitting in a showcase in a Paris restaurant. With great elation, he excitedly entered the restaurant and asked if he could purchase the pudding, but was told that it had been ordered and specifically made for an elderly customer—Monsieur de Fortgibu. Many years later, Monsieur Deschamps was invited to a dinner party where the pièce de résistance was a singular extravagance—plum pudding. After years of hunting unsuccessfully for the delicacy, Monsieur Deschamps delightedly took a generous slice and casually remarked to the company that the only thing lacking now was the presence of Monsieur de Fortgibu. At that very moment, the door opened and a very old man, frail and disoriented, walked in. It was Monsieur de Fortgibu, who had gotten hold of the wrong address and had burst in on the party by mistake!

*T*he starry Jerusalem sky seemed to portend all kinds of possibilities. Like many people, I had come to Israel on a personal pilgrimage to find something that was sorely lacking in my life. But unlike many others, I was not embarked upon a mission to find God, religion, or transcendence. I was here to find a mate.

Back in the States, all leads toward finding a spouse seemed to have fizzled out. I had been to singles parties, singles weekends, bars. Every possibility had been explored and exhausted.

My parents were frantic at having a twenty-nine-year-old unmarried daughter. I was equally unhappy.

One day, a friend told my parents that in Israel I could easily find a professional matchmaker who could help find me a husband. "Oh, but that's for the religious crowd," my parents demurred. "We're not observant."

"Don't worry," my parents' friend insisted, "there are matchmakers there for everybody! Let her give it a try."

My older single brother had been living in Israel for several years now, and he promised my parents he would look out for me. So I was shipped off by my anxious parents before I could murmur even a single word of protest.

Arriving for my first appointment with the matchmaker, I expected to find either a haggard crone or a wizened, wheezing, bent old man with a long graying beard—like a character out of *Fiddler on the Roof*— and I was not disappointed. My matchmaker wore a shapeless black dress, a fading babushka, and a toothless grin. I had to suppress a giggle when she announced her name as "Yenta." Communication was difficult, because she was not fluent in English and I spoke only a smattering of Hebrew. However, it seemed to me that the basics had been properly communicated, especially when her eyes lit up and she shouted exuberantly, "Have I got a match for you!" (really!)

"So, tell me about him," I asked eagerly.

"Well, honey," she answered, "he actually reminds me a little of you. Also American, very smart, professional, comes from a secular Jewish background like you. Let me get in touch with him and I'll call you later."

That evening, she reached me with the news that he was interested and wanted to see me right away. "Go to the little park behind the Israel museum," she said, "and he'll be waiting for you."

I gasped my astonishment at the breakneck pace of events. "Isn't he going to call me first?"

"American ways!" she retorted. "The first phone call makes only *tsuris* (trouble). You get *meshugga* (crazy) from the person's voice and then you're disappointed! Believe me, this way is much better!"

"Okay," I sighed, "what's his name?"

"His name?" she shrieked incredulously. "We don't give out names. We just tell you to meet."

"Okay," I sighed again, partly exasperated, partly overcome by the hilarity of the whole adventure. "Why can't you give me his name?"

"The Jewish world is very small!" she scolded. "If I give you his name, first thing you'll do is call a friend and ask, 'Do you know so and so?' and they'll say, 'Oh, him, are you crazy, he's not for you!' and the whole thing is spoiled. No, it's better that you shouldn't know his name until you meet him!"

"Okay," I sighed a final time. "How will I know it's him?"

"This I can tell you!" Yenta the Matchmaker shouted happily. "He'll be wearing a navy blue pinstripe suit with a red tie. He's about six feet tall and broad-shouldered. He'll be waiting for you in the Japanese Sculpture Garden."

I dressed quickly, giggling to myself as I applied my makeup in smooth, swift strokes, promising to wring my parents' necks when I saw them next. Yet, even as I chuckled over this escapade, my heart pounded just a little bit faster than usual, my eyes gleamed with an unusual brightness, and my cheeks were flushed with an uncommon glow. My skepticism was tempered by hope, an aching wish that miraculously, this unknown man would turn out to be my soul mate.

I grabbed a cab to the museum and saw the tall figure in the navy pinstripe suit waiting in the distance. His back was turned to me, but my heart lurched. He was muscular and well-built and wore his clothes with confidence. My hands trembled as I paid the taxi driver, and my knees almost buckled as I made my approach. The Jerusalem evening was cool, but small beads of sweat began to form and trickle down my face. My pulse raced. "Excuse me!" I shouted towards the figure as I advanced. "Hello . . . hello?" I called.

He wheeled around and I saw him for the first time. I had come face to face with . . . my brother!

— *Sarah Perlstein*

"*Little* children, little troubles . . . big children, big troubles!" goes an old aphorism, and ever since my teenage son began driving, I have unfortunately seen both the wisdom—and the applicability—of this timeworn saying. He's already on his second car, the first having been stolen when he forgot to lock the doors. And just last week, he called me from Long Island, where he was visiting his girlfriend, and said, in a slightly puzzled tone, "Mom? I don't know how this happened . . . but my car's been towed!" He had parked the car so that it was blocking a neighbor's driveway, and the irate man had called the police. I sighed, and advised him to call his father immediately at both his office and beeper number, and inform him of the news. He promised that he would, but clearly he hadn't, because just ten minutes later, I got a call from my husband.

Instead of sounding irate, however, he sounded oddly triumphant. Something was clearly wrong. "Honey?" he said buoyantly. "You won't believe this! I'm here in Manhattan, driving near the pier, when suddenly—of all things—I see Joey's car sailing by me—stolen by a private tow truck! Well, I said to myself, no way are you getting away with this, mister! No way am I going to let Joey's *second* car be hijacked in clear sight of me! So I quickly flagged down a police car, who called in reinforcements, and the tow truck is now surrounded by swarms of cops! Yup, I sure nailed the bastards this time!" he concluded proudly.

— *Anna Lam*

A *man* was walking along the East River promenade in New York City in a very dejected state of mind. Actually, he was more than dejected—he was suicidal, and was seriously contemplating climbing over the railing that separated the promenade from the river and throwing himself in. Life felt empty, meaningless, hollow. He felt that the writing he had devoted himself to for decades had no real value, and didn't amount to much. What had he really accomplished in life?

As he stood staring at the dark, swirling water, trying to summon up the courage to do the deed, an excited voice interrupted his thoughts. "Excuse me," said a young woman, "I'm sorry to impose upon your privacy, but aren't you Christopher D'Antonio,* the writer?" He nodded indifferently. "I hope you don't mind my approaching you, but I just had to tell you what a difference your books have made in my life! They have helped me to an incredible degree, and I just wanted to thank you."

"No, my dear, it is *I* who have to thank *you*!" D'Antonio said as he wheeled around, turned away from the East River and headed back home.

Comment:

It doesn't cost much to do a good deed. Benevolence does not have to be performed on a heroic or grandiose scale. The effect of a simple good word or a compliment can go a long way—longer than we may ever know. Sometimes, it can even save a life!

*A*s a prosperous diamond dealer, Marie Denbar's* father had outgrown his old office on Forty-seventh Street in Manhattan and had decided to rent larger quarters down the block. She was helping him move one day, when she met a neighboring merchant in front of the new place, who said casually, "Oh, it's your father who's moving in now? Well, I certainly hope he has better luck than all the previous tenants!"

"Why, what happened to them?" Marie asked, alarmed.

"Never saw a place so cursed," he muttered. "Everyone who moves in there stays one, maybe two years, then goes bankrupt. It's happened at least a dozen times."

Marie ran towards her father, who was unpacking a carton in the back of the store. "Dad, you mustn't rent this place; it brings bad luck!" And she recounted what she had just been told.

"Don't be ridiculous," Marie's father scoffed. "There's no such thing as a place having bad luck! I'm a successful businessman, and an empty space can't affect my fortunes. I'm ashamed I raised such a superstitious child."

Two years later, her father abandoned his new office, having lost, for the first time in his long career, hundreds of thousands of dollars that he was never able to recoup.

Comment:

The coincidences *could* have served as an effective warning, but unfortunately the businessman chose not to heed them. As a result, he was forced to suffer the painful consequences.

There do seem to be places that pulsate with "bad energy," whether they are homes where a terrible tragedy or act of violence took place, or storefronts that are repeatedly vacated. One would probably be well-advised to avoid these places at all costs. It is only inviting trouble and tempting fate to ignore the messages of these "coincidences."

*H*e could easily afford the air fare, but David Brody* preferred instead to drive from Montreal to New York City, which he did, on a monthly basis. Ever since an acquaintance had been killed in a small-plane crash, he had avoided air travel whenever possible. Business brought him to New York frequently, and he knew the Montreal-to-New York route by heart. He loved to drive, and often made the entire seven-hour trip in one lap, bypassing rest areas, diners, and pit stops. He drove at night, when the highway was empty and he could speed undeterred towards his destination. He had been driving effortlessly to New York for ten years now and had never once encountered any problem with the commute. He always napped on the eve of his departure, guaranteeing that he would be wakeful and alert during the journey. He adhered faithfully to this practice and often joked to friends that when he drove to New York he was "on automatic."

But one evening in May 1996, an hour into his journey from Montreal, something unusual happened to David Brody. He suddenly felt inexplicably, overwhelmingly exhausted. Every bone in his body ached with weariness, and his eyelids felt heavy with sleep. He opened the car windows, hoping that a blast of cold night air would revive him, and took a long swig of coffee from the Thermos bottle nestled on the seat next to him, but neither did the trick. He felt utterly sapped, completely enervated, totally drained. And he was puzzled, almost alarmed, by this uncommon state of affairs: In all the years he had been driving to New York, he had never once experienced difficulty. He was only an hour into his journey and, besides, he had just woken up from a four-hour nap. This overpowering weariness didn't make any sense at all. Could he be ill?

Unable to drive any longer, David pulled off at the nearest exit, heading for an all-night gas station. He found himself in a small, obscure village in upstate New York which he had never heard of and had never noticed, even in passing. "Hi, how ya doing!" a jovial gas station attendant greeted him. "What can I do you for?"

"Any motels or hotels nearby?" David asked.

"You bet," answered the attendant. "I have a list with their phone numbers. Can I get it for you?" he offered graciously.

"Thanks a lot," David answered gratefully. But when he called all the lodgings on the list, he was disappointed to learn they were all solidly booked.

"Hmm, that's real unusual!" exclaimed the helpful gas station attendant. "Tourist season doesn't begin for another two weeks!"

"Well, how about places a little further away?" David asked anxiously.

"Here's a list of motels within a fifty-mile radius," said the attendant. "I'm sure you'll find a room in one of these places."

But to the attendant's surprise and David's consternation, these too were solidly booked. "Well, I'll be darned," muttered the attendant. "That's strange!"

"Listen," David said tensely, "I'm really desperate for a place to sleep. Is there maybe a sleep-away high school or college dormitory around here that might rent me a room for the night?"

"Nope, sorry," said the attendant, "can't say there is."

"Well," David said, feeling frantic for sleep and grasping at straws, "what about an old-age home?"

"Hey, you know," said the attendant happily, "there *is* one right down the road. And the owner, Patrick Riley*, is a real nice guy. Let me give him a call for you. I'll explain the situation and if he has an empty room, I'm sure he'll rent it out to you for the night." Sure enough, there was a spare bedroom in the home and it was made available to David for a modest fee.

In the morning, refreshed and renewed from a good night's sleep, David paid Riley, thanked him profusely, and turned to leave. Almost out the door, he suddenly wheeled around and made a U-turn back to the reception desk. "I've just had a thought," he told Riley.

"Since I'm here already, maybe I could do a good deed. In addition to being a businessman, I also happen to be an ordained rabbi. Are there any Jewish residents in this home whose needs I might be able to minister to?"

"You know," Riley answered with a bemused look, "it's kinda strange you should ask. There *was* one Jewish patient here, but he died last night. Just about the same time you arrived here, as a matter of fact."

"So what are you planning to do about a funeral and burial?" David inquired.

"Well, Samuel Weinstein* was close to a hundred and outlived all his relatives. He had no next-of-kin listed on his documents, and he died without a nickel to his name. There's no Jewish cemetery around here and I think the closest one is in Albany—a good hundred miles away. So we just figured on burying him in our local Christian cemetery, which has a pauper's field reserved for these situations."

"Listen," David said urgently, "that's very nice of you, but since he was Jewish, I'm sure he would have wanted to be buried in a Jewish cemetery. I happen to have taken my station wagon with me this time—usually I drive to New York in my Corolla—and I have room in the back for a coffin. Maybe you could arrange to release the body to me, and I'll take it to New York with me for a Jewish burial."

Later that day David arrived at the offices of a prominent Jewish burial society in Brooklyn. "So terribly sorry," murmured the director. "We could gladly do a free funeral for the man, but we don't own any cemetery plots where we can bury him. Why don't you try the Jewish burial society in Queens?" But in this other heavily Jewish borough of New York City, David encountered the same problem. Here, too, the director shook his head mournfully and said, "You know, we just never anticipated a need like this before and we never made provisions for this kind of situation. I could try to raise funds from charitable organizations or individuals to buy a plot, but it might take days. I wish I could help you." But as David turned to leave, the director shouted, "Hey, wait a minute! I just remembered that someone once told me that the Jewish burial society in Washington Heights in Upper Manhattan has just such a fund. Why don't you try them?"

In Washington Heights, David finally met with success. "Yes, indeed!" exclaimed an ancient-looking man whom he found in this cluttered, dusty office. "We do have a special charitable fund that provides free funerals *and* burials for the destitute. About fifty years ago, a wealthy Jewish philanthropist in our community was concerned that the occasion might arise when Jews would die paupers or without next of kin. To address that situation, he endowed a special fund that bought burial plots for this express purpose. We have in fact several plots set aside in our cemetery that we use. I'll take care of everything," he assured David. "First things first, though—there's some paperwork that has to be done," he said, pulling out a sheaf of documents.

"What's the deceased man's name, please?" he inquired, pen poised in the air.

"Samuel Weinstein."

"Hmm," said the director, "that name sounds familiar. Mind if I take a look at the body?" he asked, heading for the station wagon.

When the director returned to the office, David noticed a small tear trickling down his cheek. "My dear friend," he announced to David, "not only will we be happy to give Samuel Weinstein a plot in our cemetery, we will give him the place of honor! God's ways are indeed mysterious, my friend. The man in the back of your station wagon happens to be none other than the very same philanthropist who originally established the Free Burial Fund. He will be laid to rest in the cemetery plot he himself purchased . . . . Your journey was long and arduous, Mr. Brody. But through your most commendable efforts, Samuel Weinstein has indeed been returned to his rightful place!"

Comment

Our actions are like a stone thrown into the river. The impact of their effects ripples on and on.

*A*llen Falby, an El Paso County highway patrolman, and Alfred Smith, a businessman, met for the first time on a hot June night when Falby crashed his motorcycle.

He was racing down the road to overtake a speeding truck when the vehicle slowed down to make a turn. Unaware that the truck was slowing, Falby slammed full throttle into its tailgate. The crack-up demolished the cycle and nearly amputated one of Falby's legs. As he lay in agony on the pavement, a pool of blood began to form beneath his shattered limb. He had ruptured an artery in his leg and was bleeding to death.

It was then that fate brought Falby and Smith together.

Smith had been driving home along the road when he saw the accident. Shaken but alert, he was out of his car and bending over the badly injured man almost before the sound of the impact died on the night air.

Smith wasn't a doctor but could see what had to be done for the dying patrolman. Whipping off his tie, Smith quickly bound Falby's leg in a crude tourniquet. It worked. The flow of blood slackened to a trickle and then stopped entirely. When the ambulance arrived a few minutes later, Smith learned for the first time that he had saved Falby's life.

Five years later, around Christmas, Falby was on highway night patrol when he received a radio call from headquarters to investigate an accident along U.S. 80. A car had smashed into a tree. A man was in serious condition, and an ambulance was on the way.

Falby reached the wreck well before the ambulance. Pushing his way past a group of frightened bystanders, he found the injured man slumped unconscious across the torn car seat.

The man's right pants leg was saturated and sticky with blood. He had severed a major artery and was bleeding to death. Well trained in first aid, Falby quickly applied a tourniquet above the ruptured artery. When the bleeding stopped, he pulled the man from the car and made him more comfortable on the ground.

That's when Falby recognized the victim. He was Alfred Smith, the man who had saved his own life five years before.

Fate had brought the two men together again—and both meetings had been for the same purpose: for one man to save the life of the other in exactly the same way.

"Well," Falby told Doug Storer of the *National Tattler*, who first reported the story, "you might say, it all goes to prove that one good tourniquet deserves another!"

Comment

When passing someone in need of help, people frequently think: "I'm busy, let someone else stop; it doesn't have to be me."

But what if the person who needs the help is really *you*, only the time hasn't come yet for you to see that so clearly?

$\mathcal{O}$*n* a glass-enclosed case in Philadelphia's Maritime Museum lies a yellowing, tattered, frayed copy of a novel published in 1898 by Morgan Robertson. The novel, a work of fiction, recounts the story of the sinking of a big, fast, and luxurious ship, delineating all the details and events leading up to what the book describes as the greatest ocean disaster in history.

In the novel, Robertson describes a colossal ship, practically a behemoth, believed to be unsinkable, embarking on its maiden voyage in the month of April. It is out to set a record, and some of the wealthiest and most influential society figures from both Europe and America are on board. It is speeding along the northern lanes of Atlantic travel when it suddenly crashes into an iceberg and goes down swiftly. An inadequate number of lifeboats—only twenty-four—are on board, and consequently there is an enormous loss of life.

The name of Robertson's fictional ship? . . . the *Titan*.

Twelve years later, in April 1912, the world-famous *Titanic* went down. The details of Robertson's story (called *The Wreck of the Titan*) paralleled the actual events of the sinking of the *Titanic* with uncanny faithfulness.

The fictional *Titan* had 3,000 persons aboard, the Titanic 2,207. Both were considered unsinkable because of their allegedly watertight compartments, and both made their maiden voyage in April. The length of the *Titan* was 800 feet, the *Titanic* was 882.5, and both used three propellers. The *Titan*'s speed at impact with the iceberg was 25 knots; the *Titanic*'s 23. The displacement tonnage of the *Titan* was 75,000 while the *Titanic*'s was 66,000. And while there was a grossly inadequate number of lifeboats aboard the fictional *Titan* — an appallingly meager twenty-four — the *Titanic* had even fewer — only twenty in all.

*F*or two years they worked in the same section at the post office. "Just another new person," she said when he transferred in.

Many nights they'd find themselves working next to each other on one of the belts, sorting envelopes in the main Philadelphia office at 30th and Market. They'd make small talk—the weather, the job—then go their own ways.

But never did the environment get personal. It took a mutual friend's questioning for postal workers Yvette "Cookie" Richardson and James Austin to realize that they were long-lost brother and sister—who had not seen each other in more than 30 years.

When he was an infant and she was a toddler, their South Philadelphia family dissolved. Since then, they have traveled separate but similar paths, going to school within blocks of each other, both studying accounting, both eventually landing among the 1,825 postal employees who work the 4 P.M. shift at 30th Street, culling Philadelphians' mail.

"Working in the same department side by side," Richardson says, shaking her head. "The same place, the same time, every day. What are the odds of that?"

Their paths started to cross one night in June, at the beginning of the shift, as Austin, 33, was talking to a

205

fellow shop steward about the movies. They got into how Austin never cried, and the steward mentioned that he was just like her friend Cookie.

The steward, Barrie Bowens, told him she even cried at funerals of people she didn't know. Austin started talking about how his father died young and he never knew his mother.

For some reason Bowens asked Austin his mother's name, and he said, Veronica Potter.

"That's Cookie's mom's name," she replied.

He told her he did have a sister, although he hadn't seen her since he was a baby. Her name was Yvette.

"That's Cookie's name," Bowens replied.

Talk to her, Austin urged Bowens. For the next several hours, his head spun as he moved the mail. He was seven months old when his father, James Austin Sr., left his mother. He was sent to live with his father's parents, who raised him in North Philadelphia. The girl, 14 months older, stayed with their mother in South Philadelphia.

Several times he had looked through the phone book under Potter for his mother, whom he met once again when he was 14. But she wasn't listed. He figured it wasn't meant to be.

About 6 P.M. that night in June, Bowens approached her friend Cookie and told her they had to talk.

According to Richardson, who is 34, Bowens managed to tread delicately around the subject, not wanting to upset her. Did she have a brother? Did she have any idea where he might be?

"I met someone," Bowens finally told her. "Would you like to meet him?"

"I'm thinking, 'Yeah, sure,'" recalled Richardson. "Where is he?"

"He's close."

"How close?"

"In Cancellation."

"Cancellation?"

Austin was getting off early that night, about 9:30 P.M., so the two women hurried down one floor. "We were jumping, running through Cancellation," Richardson said. Austin was walking behind a counter, when she saw him, sturdy and broad-backed with deep brown eyes and full cheeks, a kind face.

"Oh, my God! It is him," she said. She had an old picture of their father and the resemblance was suddenly startling. Austin was named after his father, and Richardson remembered how he had been called Little Jimmy.

They grabbed each other and wouldn't let go. Neither brother nor sister cried. Bowens did.

Since then, their story has moved like priority mail around the post office, where 4,100 people work. Yesterday they were standing next to each other again, posing for pictures, giving interviews above the din of metal carts rattling along concrete floors.

On a Saturday last month, in scorching heat, Richardson and her mother drove to Southwest Philadelphia, where Austin lives with his family. The three were together for the first time in more than 30 years.

His wife entertained graciously, Richardson said. Austin found the reunion to be easier than he had anticipated. "I thought it would be real awkward, but it wasn't," he said.

He said he and his mother talked for a long time, dealing gently with difficult subjects. "She did tell me she was young at the time and already had one child," Austin said.

He and his sister caught up on their lives, and they realized they had a few more things in common. She was at Girls High School the same time he was next door at Central. Both have studied accounting. They have similar senses of humor and like the same sort of movies, their co-workers tell them. Co-workers see it more than the brother and sister do.

In fact, about a year ago, one of the 30th Street workers asked Austin if Richardson was his sister. He said no, never thinking twice about it—until a few weeks ago.

"We're still getting to know each other," Austin said. They take their breaks together and talk.

"We're basically trying to establish a friendship," she said. "He's a nice person." She had never sought to find her brother, figuring he had a right to his own life. "You hope he's happy and say, 'Maybe one day . . . ' "

Comment

That which we hope for, dream about, long for and seek, may not be far off from ourselves. Finding it may simply require a mere look over the shoulder, a glance into our very own backyard, a deeper knowledge of the person standing by our side.

s the owner of The Better Half, a plus-size specialty shop in Brooklyn that has been in existence for thirteen years, I have come to know and love my customers, most of whom are "repeats." Even though they often vow to me that this is the last time they'll be shopping for large sizes because they're enrolling in a gym . . . starting a new diet . . . beginning therapy . . . working with a hypnotist— almost all of them come back regularly. I say this, not with disdain, but tenderly, with affection. I myself am a large-size woman and know the struggle.

Susan Bailey* was a "repeat" customer. An executive with a big real estate company in Manhattan, she would dart into the store twice a year (always in a big hurry), throw suits over her arm (she never tried them on, asserting that she was a perfect size 20 and knew already which cuts of which companies fit her), dash up to the counter to pay, and sprint out to a waiting car. She always went for the best: Jones New York and Harve Benard were her favorites, and she consistently ran up a tab that totaled well over a thousand dollars. Needless to say, I would get an adrenaline rush whenever she would hurtle through the door (thousand-dollar customers are not easy to come by these days) and would give her my devoted attention. Even though it was hard for me to keep up with her frenetic pace as she sped through the store, I faithfully followed her and serviced her every need, panting for minutes after she had made her hasty exit. Despite the fact that she created a hurricane in her wake, I was always delighted when she arrived. I was gratified that a big-time executive from Manhattan would patronize my humble store, even though I knew it was my huge discounts on designer clothes that were the draw, and not my sparkling personality. I was flattered anyway.

One day, I was reflecting about the customers I hadn't seen for a while, when I suddenly realized that Susan Bailey hadn't been around for a long time. A *very* long time, I thought with a start. Maybe even two years. I wondered what had happened to her. Had she been one of the minority who had gone on a successful diet and maintained her weight loss? Had she moved away? Had someone in the store insulted her unknowingly? Was she shopping somewhere else? I thought of calling her, but didn't want to be pushy. Nonetheless, I sent her a postcard announcing a special sale. It came back marked "Addressee Unknown." I felt a twinge of loss when the postcard was returned—where had Susan disappeared to . . . and why?

Every now and then, I leave the store to check out the competition. I make the rounds of all the plus-size stores in Manhattan, trying to spot trends, see which designers are hot, discover new labels. I make these forays two or three times a year. I was on just this kind of expedition one day, and was peering into the windows of Jeanne

Rafal, a large-size specialty shop opposite Lord & Taylor on Fifth Avenue, when I heard a plaintive voice behind me. "Please, Ma'am, can you spare some change?" I wheeled around to face my petitioner. My jaw dropped open in astonishment and disbelief. It was Susan Bailey.

Gone were the Jones New York suit, the chic haircut, the flawless makeup. In the place of the woman I had known stood a stranger, disheveled, unwashed, and disoriented. "Susan!" I shrieked. "What's happened to you?"

She didn't seem to recognize me. "Please Ma'am," she repeated piteously, "can you spare some change?"

I pulled out all the money in my wallet and gave her forty dollars. As she stood looking at the bounty in her hand with delight, I gazed at her, stricken. "Susan," I said gently, "let's go somewhere to eat and talk." She shook her head no. "Susan," I said again, "don't you remember me . . . The Better Half of Brooklyn?"

For a moment, the cloudy eyes cleared. "Oh, yeah, sure," she said.

"Susan . . . what's happened?" I asked softly in what I hoped was a matter-of-fact manner, trying to conceal my shock and pain at her condition.

"Oh . . ." she muttered vaguely, "the real estate market went bust . . . I lost my job . . . my mother died . . . my brother stole my inheritance and kicked me out of our house . . . all kinds of terrible things."

"Where are you living now?"

"In a shelter," she mumbled, embarrassed. Then, just as suddenly as it had appeared, the spark of intelligence that had gleamed briefly in her eyes dimmed, and she became muddled and confused again.

"Susan, would you like to come stay in my house for awhile? I have a finished basement where you could live comfortably," I offered.

"No, no, no," she said, starting to back away, looking at me with suspicion. "I have to leave now; I have an appointment. I have to go!"

"Susan!" I pleaded, running after her. "I want to help you. Here's my number—please call me." Apathetically, she took my card.

"Susan," I pressed, "will you call me?"

"Sure, sure," she muttered, retreating quickly.

But she never did.

— *Yitta Halberstam Mandelbaum*

Comment:

Can life change so quickly? The owner of The Better Half was haunted and traumatized by this encounter, and thought about it for years afterward. She learned never to take the abundance in her life for granted. And yet, even while she came to cherish her blessings and to thank God for them, she also became mindful of how very transient they truly are.

*S*everal years ago, I treated my two grandchildren to dinner at a fast-food restaurant on Avenue J in Brooklyn, in a thriving shopping district. Although it is now closed, at that time a movie theatre adjoined the restaurant, and my grandchildren happened to notice the marquee as we passed by. It was displaying the name of a popular Disney movie, one my grandchildren hadn't yet seen. Needless to say, almost as soon as they began tearing into their burgers, they began campaigning to see the movie. Unfortunately, I had spent all my money on dinner, and literally didn't have a penny left. I tried to explain this to them, but they were very young and didn't understand. In fact, they began to wail in such a heartrending way that I had to take them out of the restaurant because they were disturbing the other diners.

On the street corner, I went through my pocketbook over and over again, checking every zippered compartment, shaking out every paper, hoping against hope that I would find a ten-dollar bill hidden somewhere, which is all that I required to get us into the movie. But not an extra penny dropped into my waiting palm. As the children's persistent crying rose to a shrill crescendo, I frantically turned every pocket of both the coat and suit I was wearing inside out, but again my efforts were in vain. Nothing. The cacophony of cries issuing from the children was now high-pitched and intense. I bit my lips in distress and muttered to myself in quiet desperation, "Oh, God. If I only had ten dollars. What I wouldn't give for ten dollars right this minute!"

Suddenly, to my shock and astonishment, dollar bills started floating down—seemingly from the sky—fluttering and landing at my feet. Stunned, I looked up at the second-story windows of the store buildings on the street, certain that someone holding the money had looked out a window and inadvertently dropped it. However, no anxious face peered out of any window, and no hastening figure hurried out of any building to retrieve the cash.

Stupefied, I bent down to pick up the dollars, which totaled ten in all—exactly the amount I needed for the tickets—one adult, two children!

I waited for about fifteen minutes to see if anyone would appear to claim the money. When nobody did, and I had satisfied my moral impulse to try to see that the money was rightfully returned, I took the children in tow and headed for the movie. In my head, I thanked my unknown and mysterious benefactor. I paid for the tickets, and went into the theatre. The movie was just about to begin.

— *Ettie Grossman*

Comment

With God, we are co-creators of our existence and destiny. When we declare for ourselves what we want in life, this declaration somehow goes into a law of mind and comes back to us as experience. Spoken words are the foundation of what we continually create in our own lives. We should never underestimate or limit their tremendous power.

*U*nrelentingly logical, I have always been a math-science person. I graduated high school in 1970 as a math major and went to UCLA, where I received a Bachelor of Arts in Theoretical Mathematics in 1974. Then, being a practical sort who aspired to employment, I entered UCLA Dental School and graduated with a Doctorate of Dental Surgery four years later. At that time, I had fully intended to pursue a career as a dentist. One doesn't usually attend dental school for self-actualization.

That was twenty-two years ago. And during those past twenty-two years, I've never picked up a drill—euphemistically known as a handpiece—nor have I scraped a single tartar-coated tooth. Instead, I am now a writer of detective fiction, choosing to explore the human condition instead of oral hygiene.

I couldn't pinpoint the metamorphosis, but I am glad it worked out that way. I could list several factors that steered me toward mystery writing—a desire for justice, a suspicious nature, an overactive imagination, and, of course, a penchant for the bizarre. All of the above can be summed up by what transpired the day I nabbed a mugger.

On that particular morning, my then four-year-old son—now a strapping lad of eighteen—had chosen to come down with a high fever and a burning sore throat. I suspected strep throat. My mother was at the house, lending a comforting hand while caring for my year-old daughter. Rather than drag the entire crew to the pediatrician, I suggested that my mother take a walk with the baby to the corner bakery while I ran my preschooler to the doctor's. It was a fine LA day—sunny, but not too hot. Yes, I thought, a walk would be refreshing for both Grandma and baby. Not to mention the fact that the soft-hearted bakery lady was always good for a couple of extra cookies for my tyke.

Grandma, baby, and stroller left first. I followed a few minutes later, and I could see them easily about a half-block up. As I pulled out of my driveway, I noticed a car near them but on the opposite side . . . slowing . . . then stopping. A young man got out of the front passenger's seat and started walking. And walking. And walking. Across the street from my mother and daughter, about twenty feet behind them.

But keeping pace with them.

I straightened the wheel of my automobile and shifted into drive. The car up the street was still there . . . creeping by . . . slowly.

And the man kept walking. Still across the way from my mother and child, still keeping pace.

That is odd, I thought. When I let someone out of the car, that person usually goes into a house. He doesn't keep walking for a block or two.

I'm being paranoid, I decided. Nevertheless, this was my daughter, this was my mother. I drove down the street, pointedly behind the creeping car. And then it drove away.

Just like that.

And I felt a little better.

Meanwhile, the man across the street kept strolling aimlessly, not doing anything suspicious. I waved to my mom and she waved back. Then I drove off.

But something nagged at my gut.

I turned the corner, made a series of right turns and circled around the block. Then I caught up with my mother, who was blithely ambling in the sunshine. Again, we exchanged waves, although she did have a puzzled look on her face. It said, "Why did you come back?"

And the man across the street continued to keep pace with my mother.

Too much TV, I chided myself.

Too many detective novels.

I drove off. One block, then another.

But this was my daughter, this was my mother.

Again, I retraced my steps.

By the time I returned, my mother was down on her knees, her hand gripping her head. The stroller had been tipped over. My heart raced as I pulled over, screaming, "Are you all right?"

"He took my purse," she shouted hysterically.

Frantically, she pointed around the corner.

Again, I asked if she was all right. Was the baby all right?

Yes, my mother answered. Despite the fact that she had two scraped knees from her fall, she was fine.

Anger coursed through my body. This was my *baby*, this was my *mother*!

With my son firmly ensconced in his car seat, I gave chase. Admittedly, not the brightest decision I've made. But I reacted rather than considered.

The French Connection it wasn't. I was in a car and he was on foot, so I caught up rather handily. Learning on the horn, I rolled down the window and screamed at the top of my lungs, "Drop the purse, you son of a bitch!"

"Son of a bitch!" my son imitated from the back seat.

But the sucker kept running. In retrospect, I think it was more in fear than in obstinacy. He pumped his legs hard and fast, racing with the wind. *Chariots of Felony*. But even Jesse Owens wouldn't have had a chance against a V-8 engine. I kept honking the horn, shrieking at him to drop the goddamn purse.

"Goddamn purse," my son aped.

Up ahead was a pedestrian. Two of them. I don't remember much about them. Except that they were male and one of them was wearing a yellow plaid sports coat. I don't know why that particular fact registered, but it did. And it was the one in the plaid coat who pulled out the gun . . . pointed it at the runner and yelled "Freeze!"

And the man froze.

Just like in the movies.

I jerked the car into a driveway, not really understanding what was going on.

Plaid Coat instructed the runner to drop the purse. "Drop it," he shouted. "Drop it, drop it, drop it!"

The runner had that deer-in-the-headlights look on his face. He dropped the purse.

Plaid Coat told him to hit the ground.

Just like in the movies.

I bounded out of the car, spoke to Plaid Coat. I pointed to the runner, pointed to my mother's stolen handbag and angrily said, "That's not his purse!"

Neighbors began filing out, offering to call the police. Which was kind of redundant.

Because Plaid Coat had turned out to be an off-duty policeman who had been visiting his father, heard me leaning on the horn, and came out to investigate.

Now he took off his belt and began to secure the suspect. At that point, I went back to my mother. She was upright and so was the stroller. I pulled the car over, loaded them both inside. Her palms were sore, her pants were ripped at the knees. But as promised, both she and my baby were all right.

"He took my purse!" my mother sobbed.

"We caught him, Ma," I said.

"You what?"

"We caught him. We have your purse!"

"Oh. that's good," my mother answered. "That's very good."

"Very good," my son coughed from the back seat.

We returned to the scene of the crime, now thick with patrol cars. I explained my story as I held my baby, and my mother explained her story from inside of my car. The uniformed police officers were amazed.

"We never catch these guys," one of them told me.

My mother was required to come down to the station to claim the purse. It would be there waiting for her. The police only needed a couple of hours to process the paperwork.

"She can't just take it now?" I asked. "Save us both a trip?"

"Nope. Evidence."

"Fine," I said.

They congratulated me. I took my mother and baby home. We were all pretty shaken, but life does go on.

I loaded my son back into his car seat and zipped him over to the pediatrician. A good move on my part.

Indeed, it was strep throat.

— *Faye Kellerman*

Comment

This story by bestselling author Faye Kellerman vividly exemplifies the maxim "God helps those who helps themselves." It is probably correct to assume that many people finding themselves in the exact same situation would have been far more passive than Ms. Kellerman, who admirably assumed a proactive stance here. Although other people would have undoubtedly turned their attention towards helping their mother and child off the sidewalk and uttered a silent prayer of thanks that both had escaped harm, they probably would not have doggedly pursued the mugger until he was tagged by the undercover cop. Was the sudden and miraculous appearance of "Plaid Jacket" a mere fluke, or was it God coming on board to assist Faye, to repay her for her determination that the miscreant who preyed on elderly ladies and helpless toddlers be brought to justice? Thankfully, through her tenacious efforts, he was!

Permissions

Acknowledgments

We have been blessed with the most wonderful editor, Pamela Liflander, whose expert advice, gentle wisdom, and intelligent counsel greatly enriched our experience. Virginia Rubens, copy editor par excellence, did a superb job with our material. Elise Bauman's editorial contributions were also extremely valuable. We are very grateful to all three, whose combined efforts produced this work. We also want to thank our agents, Carol Mann and Channa Taub, for bringing our book to Adams and helping turn our dream into reality.

Judith would like to thank her father of blessed memory, Harry B. Frankel, whose broad intellect, robust humor, and richly colorful personality left a lasting impression. Her mother, Rose, lent her creativity, devotion, and uncompromising love. Her older sister Hedy and husband, Myer Feiler, and their children provided great warmth and a generous spirit. Her younger sister, Estee, has been a blessing in every way. Isser and Malku Handler are like a second set of parents and have contributed generously. Anne Leventhal defies the stereotype of mother-in-law, and provides a profound sense of support. Pessi Dinnerstein has continuously pointed onward and upward with her insights and encouraging words.

Yitta would like to thank Charles Mandelbaum, who was extremely generous, especially for repeated intrusions into his law office to use his computer, copier, and fax. Rabbi Meir Fund graciously spent time discussing the theological implications of coincidences. Miriam Halberstam, world traveler and devoted sister, scouted coincidence stories for us wherever she went.

Lastly, we wish to thank our husbands, Mordechai Mandelbaum and Jules Leventhal, who added their deep wisdom, extreme patience, kindness, and generosity of spirit, which gave us the love and support we needed to grow and complete this project.

Visit Our Website

http://www.adamsmedia.com/smallmiracles

Send us your own small miracles: Have you ever experienced an unusual, heartwarming, or mysterious coincidence? We would like to hear about these personal events, and possibly use them for an upcoming sequel. Visit our website and tell us about your small miracle. All submissions will become the property of Adams Media Corporation.

About the Authors

Yitta Halberstam has been published in over 50 national newspapers and magazines and is the author of one other nonfiction book. She has worked as a newspaper reporter, public relations director, college lecturer, high school teacher, and press aide. Currently she is employed as a Director of Special Events and Programming for a nonprofit women's organization.

Judith Frankel Leventhal, C.S.W. is a psychotherapist in private practice and lectures widely on a variety of subjects.